THE

WHITE

HOUSE

PLUMBERS

THE
WHITE
HOUSE
PLUMBERS

The SEVEN WEEKS
THAT LED TO WATERGATE
and Doomed
Nixon's Presidency

EGIL "BUD" KROGH
AND MATTHEW KROGH

ST. MARTIN'S GRIFFIN
NEW YORK

Published in the United States by St. Martin's Griffin, an imprint of St. Martin's
Publishing Group

THE WHITE HOUSE PLUMBERS. Copyright © 2022 by Matthew Krogh. All rights reserved.
Printed in the United States of America. For information, address St. Martin's Publishing
Group, 120 Broadway, New York, NY 10271.

www.stmartins.com

Library of Congress Cataloging-in-Publication Data

Names: Krogh, Egil, 1939–2020, author. | Krogh, Matthew D., author.
Title: The White House Plumbers : the seven weeks that led to Watergate and
    doomed Nixon's presidency / Egil "Bud" Krogh, and Matthew Krogh.
Description: First St. Martin's Griffin edition. | New York : St. Martin's
    Griffin, 2022. | Includes index. |
Identifiers: LCCN 2021057159 | ISBN 9781250851628 (trade paperback) |
    ISBN 9781250851635 (ebook)
Subjects: LCSH: United States—Politics and government—1969–1974. | Krogh,
    Egil, 1939–2020. | United States. White House. Special Investigations
    Unit—History. | Presidents—United States—Staff—Biography. | Nixon,
    Richard M. (Richard Milhous), 1913–1994. | Pentagon Papers.
Classification: LCC E855 .K77 2022 | DDC 973.924—dc23/eng/20211129
LC record available at https://lccn.loc.gov/2021057159

Our books may be purchased in bulk for promotional, educational, or business
use. Please contact your local bookseller or the Macmillan Corporate and
Premium Sales Department at 1-800-221-7945, extension 5442, or by email at
MacmillanSpecialMarkets@macmillan.com.

A version of this book, titled *Integrity: Good People, Bad Choices, and Life Lessons from the
White House,* was published in 2007 in the United States by PublicAffairs, a member of
the Perseus Books Group.

First St. Martin's Griffin Edition: 2022

10   9   8   7   6   5   4   3   2   1

To Egil "Bud" Krogh,
whose greatest wish was for each of us to have
the integrity to make the next right choice
(August 3, 1939–January 18, 2020)

CONTENTS

PREFACE

In my dining room at home in Bellingham, Washington, I still have the brown leather recliner that Dad bought so he could be more comfortable while we worked on this book together. It's faded from the sun and slightly crackly, much like the older recliner my brother Peter still has, one that Dad brought back to Washington State from our time in Washington, D.C. Dad passed in January 2020, and atonement for his impact on America, on the executive branch, on the rest of us, was a core theme of his life since getting out of prison in 1974.

Dad was an animated and compelling storyteller, and a person who thought deeply about his moral compass and the implications of choices he had made. In 2006, when we started this book in earnest after successfully finding a publisher with our wildly talented agent (and, full disclosure, Bud's stepdaughter and my stepsister Laura Dail), the theme was different than it is now. Then, the theme was more focused on personal atonement.

But as the book took shape, the key question of *why* one might end up searching for atonement became the focus. The answer: a loss of integrity. In a 1974 article in *Redbook* by my mom, Suzanne, she recounts our family's experiences during the Watergate period and her frequently confirmed first impression of Dad as "a highly intelligent man with a wry sense of humor and, most important, as a man of integrity." Dad had all kinds of metaphors for integrity—the hull of a boat, the shell of an egg, others more far-flung. But he spent years, decades, trying to understand why his own integrity was breached and eventually understood the long and painful process required to patch the hull of a boat that feels like it may never float again.

From meeting President Nixon in the Oval Office to his reinstatement to the bar ten years later, when he regained the privilege of practicing law after the most public of all scandals, Dad lived a journey that would be unlikely for anybody. But the lessons of what happened, how someone so driven by their own sense of right could go so wrong, feel universal. For Dad, both bookends were beginnings: The first beginning, the first bookend, was his meeting with Nixon to begin public life, a time when he took his own integrity for granted. After ten years, and the second bookend, he had a new beginning when he knew he could never again take his own integrity for granted.

Much of this book was written in a small office in my garage, as we talked through which aspects of his story made the most sense to include and, especially, which components contributed most to the core lesson about protecting one's own personal integrity from sometimes overwhelming forces. After Dad's passing, as HBO considered the possibility of basing a production on this work, Laura and I did more research into historical details to add. Some of the expanded story comes from Dad's perspective, using contemporaneous quotes and notes from our conversations; other details are mined from memories of family members.

I don't think as a child I had any real understanding of the magnitude of Watergate, or of Dad's role and his public exposure. Even during the writing of the book, as we researched details to make sure we got them right, as we discussed what happened with Daniel Ellsberg, I still didn't quite feel the importance. But as we did additional research in recent years, letters to the editor during Dad's various reinstatement hearings surfaced. The passion that people expressed in print in the late 1970s—much negative, a lot positive—make some of today's internet comments sections look tame by comparison. Those letters really shaped my sense of the personal impact that Dad and the Watergate scandals had on so many people at the time.

What you are about to read is a compact story, almost exclusively told through one man's lens. Within every chapter, if you're looking, you'll find familiar stories and plot twists that you see in other, parallel narratives. The larger stories of Daniel Ellsberg and the Pentagon Papers, Watergate, the CIA, U.S.-Cuban relations, the towering personality of Nixon—these are sprawling and immense. But I—we, including Dad—hope that this one focused perspective can shed some light on decision-making gone awry under high pressure and in secret, as well as explain one facet of the scandals that brought down the Nixon presidency.

Matthew Krogh, 2022

THE
WHITE
HOUSE
PLUMBERS

PROLOGUE

I first met President Richard Nixon in February 1971 in the Oval Office, when John Ehrlichman brought me in to meet my new boss. I last saw Nixon in 1976 in San Clemente more than six years later, after a series of scandals gripped the nation; after he won a wildly successful presidential re-election; after his subsequent resignation from the office of the presidency; and after a deep shift in Americans' faith in the executive branch of the U.S. government.

I have held myself to blame, in part, for creating the conditions for the downfall of Nixon's presidency. There were other players to be sure, many motivated by upright ideals, others less so, who were prosecuted and convicted for interrelated parts of the package of scandals that came to be known as Watergate. It remains the case, however, that during seven weeks of secret work in 1971, my group and I undermined the foundations of Nixon's presidency. We went too far in our pursuit of what we believed to be critically important breaches of national security. And in time, we would pay.

At that time in 1971, David Young and I were codirecting the "Plumbers," a secret White House group more formally known as the Special Investigations Unit, or SIU. The president had tasked us with stopping leaks of top secret information related to the Vietnam War, the Strategic Arms Limitation Talks (SALT I), and other sensitive foreign policy operations. We believed then that these leaks constituted a national security crisis and needed to be plugged at all costs. But we were wrong, and the price paid by the country was too high.

For years I pondered the reasons I committed a serious crime as codirector of the Plumbers. Our seven-week investigation targeted what we believed to be a serious national security threat—Dr. Daniel Ellsberg's leak of the top secret Pentagon Papers to *The New York Times*—and culminated in the break-in of the office of his psychiatrist, Dr. Lewis Fielding. This crime and several others that followed, including the Watergate break-in and the illegal efforts to cover it up, eventually doomed the Nixon presidency. The break-in and burglary of Dr. Fielding's office was the seminal event in the chain of events that led to Nixon's resignation on August 8, 1974.

Those seven weeks during the summer of 1971 that

doomed the Nixon presidency were not the only cause of that political tragedy. However, the burglary set a precedent that two members of the Plumbers could rely on when planning and executing the Watergate break-in in 1972. They knew that under certain circumstances, the White House staff would tolerate an illegal act to obtain information. Later, during the intensive Watergate investigations, one of the major reasons for the cover-up by President Nixon and former members of his staff was to prevent investigators from discovering information about the 1971 crime.

Extreme illegal acts were undertaken to prevent this discovery, including perjury, obstruction of justice, and the payment of hush money to the perpetrators of the 1971 crime to keep them from revealing it during the Watergate investigation. Several members of Nixon's top staff feared that discovery of the 1971 events would imperil them and the president himself. Former attorney general John Mitchell, when apprised in 1972 of what had happened in 1971, accurately described the 1971 events as the White House "horrors."

During the early years of the Nixon presidency, there was serious and lengthy discussion about using illegal means to get national security information from American citizens. On several occasions, wiretaps were placed without warrants. But the burglary of Dr. Fielding's office constituted the most extreme and unconstitutional covert action taken to that date, setting the stage for the downfall of the Nixon presidency. Once undertaken, it was an action that could not be undone or explained away.

Why did this burglary happen? I am convinced, after reading dozens of accounts by others about those times and having long conversations with friends and former colleagues, that a collapse of integrity among those of us who conspired, ordered, and carried out this action was the principal cause. We made our decisions in an emergency context. The nation faced serious foreign policy threats from the Vietnam War and the Soviet Union, while the White House staff struggled with President Nixon's penchant for secrecy, his fury at those who leaked classified documents, and his orders to investigate relentlessly those individuals he felt would compromise national security.

In 1971, I firmly believed that the information we hoped to acquire from Dr. Fielding would help us prevent further leaks from undermining President Nixon's plan for ending the Vietnam War. Two and a half years later, I went to prison for approving and organizing that burglary. By then I was deeply remorseful, conflicted, and convinced that I had lost my way, a complete contrast to the ebullient good humor with which I had embarked on my great adventure in government.

Every administration brings in a huge cadre of younger staffers to fill the many crucial positions that keep the White House running. Those of us who joined the Nixon transition team to serve on Ehrlichman's and H. R. "Bob"

Haldeman's staffs had no experience with high government. For the most part, we were young businessmen and lawyers who served on the 1968 campaign staff as advance men, policy analysts, speechwriters, or media experts and who were linked professionally and personally in some way with our principals before joining the staff. Our loyalties were to our principals and to the president personally.

Long before I understood the seriousness of the many responsibilities I would be given, I was sent to New York City to work in the transition office. The Nixon transition set up shop in the Pierre hotel in New York City, one of the most elegant and expensive hotels in North America. As the Pierre was located a block away from Nixon's apartment on Fifth Avenue, the president-elect could walk to work each morning, providing numerous photo opportunities for tourists and journalists. Some of us who joined the transition staff in New York were lodged at the Wyndham Hotel, an actors' hotel, located across 57th Street from the Plaza Hotel. Like the Pierre, the Plaza was a grand place with great tradition and astronomical prices. The most famous resident of the Wyndham during the two months I lived there was the prop dog who played in the hit musical *Annie*. Like two-legged stars, this dog had a staff of handlers who tried to keep him on leash and on schedule.

I shared an office on the eleventh floor of the Pierre with Edward Morgan, an Arizona lawyer, who had also been one of Ehrlichman's most effective advance men during the campaign. When I first met Ed, he regaled me with stories from the campaign that made me feel I had missed out on one of life's great opportunities. He was a very tall, heavyset man with a bright, cherubic face. When describing the day-to-day absurdities of the campaign and local political leaders, he would explode into long riffs of increasingly off-color language that left me and anyone else within earshot helpless with laughter. He became one of my best friends over the next four years.

Ed and I were tasked to vet the stock holdings and corporate backgrounds of the president's nominees to the cabinet and sub-cabinet to make sure there were no real or apparent conflicts of interest. A federal statute prohibited an individual from holding a federal position that would enable him to benefit from that position. Not only were actual conflicts proscribed, but the appearance of conflicts was also outlawed.

One of the first sets of stocks and previous corporate responsibilities we reviewed involved the then governor of Massachusetts, John Volpe. The president had nominated the governor to be secretary of transportation. When he came to meet Ed and me, we discovered that there was a clear appearance of a conflict of interest because his privately owned company, the John Volpe Construction Company, was constructing the new Department of Transportation building in the capital. I told him we had learned there was a big sign out in front of the construction site that read, THIS BUILDING IS BROUGHT TO YOU BY THE JOHN VOLPE CONSTRUCTION COMPANY, or words to that effect. This constituted an appearance of a conflict, and we suggested that he change the name and convey all management responsibility to someone else. He agreed to do so. The governor and his lawyer returned a few days later to report on the steps they had taken. The governor said he had transferred all management tasks to his brother. We reviewed the document that showed his brother was directed under this shift in management to have no contact with the governor during his time of service at the Department of Transportation.

"That's great," I remember saying. "That should take care of the management issue. And what's the new name?"

"I've changed it to 'The Volpe Construction Company,'" he answered.

I looked at Ed, who was looking pensively at his desk. The mirthful twitching of his mouth indicated that he did not trust himself to respond.

I jumped in, trying my best to maintain a serious professional demeanor. "Well," I said, "we're getting closer. But I think the real problem, Governor, is not the first name, but the last. Perhaps you could find a name that doesn't have 'Volpe' in it."

He agreed and told his lawyer to come up with some suggestions. After concluding our financial discussion, the governor and his lawyer got up, we all shook hands, and then they left.

Our room at the Pierre was large and had been stripped of the bed and easy chairs. Ed and I faced each other while we worked, crammed in behind two large desks. Small chairs faced the sides of our desks, where the cabinet nominees and their lawyers sat while we worked through their financial histories. Three doors led from the room: one that led into the hall, one into the closet, and one into the bedroom. After winding up our vetting session with one cabinet-position nominee, who shall remain nameless, Ed and I turned around and moved over to sit down at our desks. We sensed the nominee turn around and, without hesitation, walk confidently into the closet, closing the door behind him. Ed and I looked at each other briefly, picked up some papers, and pretended to read through them. Had the man emerged immediately there wouldn't have been a problem. But he delayed, excruciatingly.

Time stretched out as slowly as I can ever remember. A quick glance showed that Ed's face was becoming redder and redder. I felt my eyes begin to water, and to keep from letting any weird sounds come out, I started biting the inside of my mouth. Finally—it seemed forever—we noticed out of our peripheral vision the knob on the closet door begin to turn ever so slowly. Then, as we continued to look at our papers and not toward the nominee, he slowly exited through the closet door and oozed along the wall to the other door, opened it gently, and tiptoed into the hall.

Ed exploded. He started laughing and sobbing so hard I thought he would choke. His head dropped down to his arms folded on his desk. My eyes were drowning in tears. I leaned back so far in my chair that I fell off onto the floor, where I sat gently banging my head against the wall. The high farce completely wiped out any prospect of further work that day.

"Twenty-seven fucking seconds," Ed managed. "That's how long he was in there."

To let loose our pent-up hilarity, we rushed out of the Pierre that afternoon, took a left turn, and for the next two hours walked up and down Fifth Avenue singing Broadway musical tunes. We belted out songs from *Oklahoma!*, *The King and I*, *Showboat,* and whatever else came into our crazed minds. Christmas shoppers scurrying along Fifth must have concluded that we had started drinking hours earlier. We were part of the new government of the most powerful nation on earth, and it felt like the beginning of an exuberant journey in which we were all destined to ride high.

Four years later, the transformation could hardly have been more complete. The laughter lasted barely into 1969, and in its place a very different mood took hold. The mood was darker, less open, more anxious, more defensive. I was never again to be so happy-go-lucky in government as that afternoon at the Pierre allowed me to be.

EACH OF THE commissions that I was given during my time in the White House came with a handsomely framed certificate that included the phrase "reposing special trust in

your integrity." At the time, I thought nothing of the ter-
minology; it seemed like governmental jargon, a way to
make the process of taking a job more august. But in the
years since, I came back to the language of those commissions and found in it a more subtle and far-reaching moral
imperative. I skipped across it as a young man; later, I came
to believe that integrity is one of the most important personal qualities that any individual in a position of power
or responsibility can show, whether in business, politics, or
public and private life. Trying to understand what integrity really means in those commissions helped me develop
a framework for my own life and gave me a way of seeing
how others in the pressure of competitive environments
could avoid doing what I did. Because if you compromise
your integrity, you allow a little piece of your soul to slip
through your hands. Integrity, like trust, is all too easy to
lose, all too difficult to restore.

Few who knew me in 1970 would have considered me
as the sort of person who would break a law for any reason whatsoever. Raised in a highly moral family, provided
with an excellent education including law school and the
Navy, my values were those of Christian Middle America. Money, outside influences, the system itself can all
be sources of the sort of corruption that infects politics.
The same can be said for elements of the business world
or any other competitive environment. I am now not the
same man that I was as a twenty-nine-year-old, fresh-faced
young man in government with the whole world appar-

ently ahead of him. Sometimes I hardly recognize that younger man. It makes it easier to see his actions and decisions, for better or worse, in some kind of perspective. The young Bud Krogh wanted to do the right thing, but the correct path wasn't always clear to him. A combination of youthful naivete, ambition, loyalty, and a military sense of duty—each a virtue in the right proportion—was his undoing when mixed with the rarer elements of a career in the White House against the fever-pitched backdrop of the Vietnam War.

My friend Lynn Sutcliffe wrote the following to the judge before I was sentenced to prison in 1974:

> In most situations Bud's commendable character traits would have caused him to disapprove the commission of an illegal act. The events surrounding the Fielding break-in played upon those usually commendable traits in such a way as to produce the opposite result. But to understand Bud's actions is not to excuse or condone them.

By describing the circumstances around what happened in 1971, and the tumultuous events in American society at the time, I certainly don't mean to excuse or condone my actions. I still deeply regret my actions, which worked a destructive force upon our nation. These actions and the efforts to cover them up led to widespread distrust in our government and its leaders that continues to this day. I do, however, mean to provide a partial explanation of how somebody like myself—somebody with all the advantages, somebody meaning to do well—can commit a crime not by accident, mind you, but by skewed priorities, misplaced loyalties, overwhelming external pressures, and clouded judgment.

During my time in the White House, there were many temptations or ideas that could have waylaid any of us. Ideologies, alliances, power, the ability to do good for the country and the world, all combined into a nearly intoxicating work and life environment. This story starts with a decision in the high summer of 1971, the consequences of which were quite different than any of us had foreseen.

1

TWO DECISIONS IN TWO DAYS

On July 15 and 17, 1971, President Richard M. Nixon made two critical national security decisions. The first decision will go down in the history books as one of the boldest acts of diplomacy in the twentieth century. The second decision, which embroiled me in more personal difficulties than I could ever have imagined, led to the downfall of the Nixon presidency.

I had been at an impromptu visit by Nixon to the Lincoln Memorial at 4:45 A.M. on May 9, 1970, a few days after he had decided to invade Cambodia. During an hour-long discussion with a group of stunned students who had come to protest his actions, he told them he had "great hopes that during my administration . . . the great mainland of China would be opened up so that we could know the 700 million people who live in China, who are one of the most remarkable people on earth." That foreshadowing of his intention to open China finally climaxed with his electrifying announcement to the world on July 15, 1971.

On the evening of that day, the president told the world that on July 1, Dr. Henry Kissinger had conducted secret talks with Premier Zhou Enlai of China, during which Zhou invited Nixon to visit China "before May 1972." The president said he had accepted Zhou's invitation with pleasure. His subsequent visit to China in February 1972, hinted at in his writings and numerous comments over the previous four years, constituted the most dramatic and, to knowledgeable experts in U.S. foreign policy, the most significant achievement of the Nixon presidency.

But on the morning of July 17, the president made a second, very different decision. That morning he presided over a meeting that I attended on the patio outside his office at the so-called western White House in San Clemente, California. The western White House included the president's home, La Casa Pacifica, an ornate white-stuccoed and red-tiled building that was located just to the north of a small, one-story office building complex that contained offices for the president, senior staff, and the traveling White House entourage. La Casa Pacifica, perched on the bluffs above the best surfing beach in Southern California, had a magnificent view. The president purchased it in 1969, and it had become his residence when he took extended vacations away from Washington, D.C.

The view from the patio outside the president's office was also spectacular, and we could see a U.S. Navy destroyer steaming through the whitecaps just off the coast in the bright morning sunshine, providing security for the president and his family. La Casa Pacifica's office complex was located just to the north of the Camp Pendleton Marine Corps base. With the Marines to the south, the Navy to the west, and the Secret Service embedded in various posts around the western White House, the president lived and worked in a sort of militarized high-security resort.

A May 1971 congressional report highlighted the difficulties facing our troops in Vietnam: boredom and stress had led many to turn to drugs—marijuana and heroin among them. The problem worsened when an influx of inexpensive high-potency heroin hooked around one-fifth of the troops at some point during their tours of Vietnam. The growing heroin epidemic in Vietnam, and spikes in crime from addicted soldiers returning home, was a key aspect of Nixon's June 1971 declaration that drug abuse is "public enemy number one in the United States," beginning the modern phase of the "war on drugs." The purpose of the July 17 meeting was to report to the president on the progress of a major administration effort he had launched a few weeks before to curb the use of heroin by our soldiers in Vietnam.

Except for the president and counsel and assistant to the president for domestic affairs, Ehrlichman, the other meeting attendees—Dr. Jerome Jaffe, Dr. Beny Primm, and I—were jet-lagged from our respective trips. We sat around a glass patio table, enjoying the sunshine as we presented the president with a thorough report on our findings. The president looked tanned and rested, and his mood was ebullient, the result of the overwhelmingly positive response to his China announcement two nights before.

I had just returned the day before from two weeks of travel to France, Greece, Turkey, India, Thailand, Laos, and South Vietnam, where I was assessing the effectiveness of our international narcotics control programs in these countries. The results were mixed, with good results in curbing the growth of poppies in Turkey but less success in preventing the flow of heroin into South Vietnam. During my trip I had met with action officers in the State Department, the CIA, the Bureau of Narcotics and Dangerous Drugs, the U.S. Customs Service, and the U.S. Military Assistance Command, Vietnam, telling all of them about the president's strong commitment to reducing the flow of illegal drugs into the United States.

My final foreign stop on the two-week trip was in South Vietnam, where I joined up with Dr. Jaffe, the newly designated chief of the Special Action Office for Drug Abuse Prevention; Seth Rosenberg, Dr. Jaffe's assistant; and Dr. Primm, one of Jaffe's principal drug treatment advisers. They met me in South Vietnam so that we could take a firsthand look at the urinalysis centers the military had recently set up at the president's direction in Long Binh and Cam Ranh Bay. The machines in these centers tested for the presence of opiates in soldiers' urine. If soldiers tested positive, they would need to go through treatment before being released into civilian life. Long Binh and Cam Ranh Bay were the principal debarkation centers for U.S. soldiers leaving Vietnam following their tours of duty. The handmade sign above the entrance to the center at Long Binh proclaimed its purpose: THE PEE HOUSE OF THE AUGUST MOON.

During our trip in South Vietnam, we also had visited several military facilities, met with commanders and their staffs, and observed the functioning of the diagnostic system. In our meetings, we became acutely aware of the toll the war was taking on our soldiers, and we promised to provide all the help we could. We were encouraged to learn that the diagnostic system we had just instituted showed less opiate use by our soldiers than we had expected. In our meeting with the president, we reported the findings that the number of U.S. military personnel who tested positive for opiates in their systems, approximately 4.5 percent, was well below the 20 percent figure reported in the press. The president told us how pleased he was with the results so far and encouraged us to move ahead aggressively with the program. He said he was glad that the percentages showed that 96 percent of those who came back from Vietnam could be employed and move back into society without fear of them being drug users. Following this meeting with the president, Dr. Jaffe, Dr. Primm, and I briefed the television pool reporters on the meeting and the results of the trip.

What gave me the most satisfaction that day was the conviction that our Vietnam drug program would help us alleviate the false perception among some Americans, especially business leaders, that the Vietnam veteran was a ruthless killer, a junkie, and therefore unemployable. The president was committed to changing the image of the Vietnam vet as a junkie. He had told me and others in a previous meeting on June 3, 1971, that narcotics would be an issue used by adversaries to his Vietnam policy to impugn the military, so it was both a political and a real issue. With the number of positive tests among our soldiers lower than what we had anticipated, I felt we had made a solid contribution to defending against any opposition to the president's Vietnam policy based on the narcotics issue. Following lunch at the western White House with Dr. Jaffe, I was feeling very good about what we had accomplished and was looking forward to some rest and relaxation before returning to D.C. But this was not to be. Ehrlichman's secretary found me and said that he wanted to see me as soon as it was convenient. This always meant immediately.

When I was waved in to Ehrlichman's office, he got up and quietly closed the door behind me. This surprised me because his office was already in the innermost sanctum of offices closest to the president's own. Any additional secrecy afforded by a closed door didn't seem necessary to me at the time. Then he told me about the president's second national security decision.

I sat down in a chair in front of his desk and he handed me a bulky file labeled PENTAGON PAPERS, the colloquial name for the *Report of the Office of the Secretary of Defense Vietnam Task Force*. I leafed through the contents, which included newspaper reprints of the Pentagon Papers, news stories about the papers and about the Supreme Court's rejection of the government's request to restrain their publication, and various internal memos. As I read, Ehrlichman told me that the assignment he was about to give me had been deemed of the highest national security importance by the president. He emphasized that the president was as angry about the leak of the Pentagon Papers as he had ever seen him on any other issue.

In his dry style, Ehrlichman said that while I was junketing around the world working on drug programs and policies, he, along with White House chief of staff Bob Haldeman, then head of the National Security Council Kissinger, and special counsel to the president Chuck Colson had been working hard and meeting regularly with the president to determine how best to respond to the leak of the Pentagon Papers, which he described as a "crisis." According to Ehrlichman, the president was certain that a conspiracy was involved in the release of the Pentagon Papers and that we needed to run our own investigation to find out who was part of the conspiracy. He said the president didn't believe that a thorough investigation could be carried out by the FBI or the Department of Justice. Consequently, he had ordered that an independent White House team be set up to begin its own investigation immediately. This new team would investigate the ramifications of the release of the Pentagon Papers to the press by Daniel Ellsberg. Ellsberg had served in the Marines, earned a Ph.D. from Harvard, and worked for the RAND Corporation, where he was one of a few employees to have access to a 7,000-page highly classified report about the history of the Vietnam War. Given his lofty credentials and the threat posed by his access to classified documents, the investigation was to have the highest priority, and preparations were to begin that day.

Ehrlichman told me a decision had also been made to share responsibility for the Pentagon Papers investigation between a representative from Kissinger's National Security Council staff and one from Ehrlichman's Domestic Council staff. Ehrlichman had assigned me to be a codirector of the investigation, and Kissinger had assigned Young, one of his closest personal aides, to be the other codirector. All personal and written reports were to go to Ehrlichman, who was to be the channel to the president. He told me that Colson would assign someone from his group to work with us as well.

It was a lot to digest in one short meeting. The idea of making a team—soon to be known as the Special Investigations Unit (SIU)—out of three people drawn from three different staffs, each person with primary loyalty to his respective boss, seemed to me to be at best unwieldy if not impossible to manage effectively. I did not express any misgivings to Ehrlichman at the time, however, since I felt that this was the most critical assignment I had yet been given on Nixon's staff, and it was not for me to question the wisdom of the structure.

Nixon's White House staff comprised several individual fiefdoms. Staff members were chosen on the basis of loyalty to the president and to the senior presidential aide who had recruited him or her. This created independent chains of loyalty—effectively clans—all the way up to the president. While there was regular communication, cooperation, and endless meetings among the staffs, there was no doubt about the senior staff person to whom a junior staff member owed primary allegiance. This resulted in a less cohesive and monolithic White House than most people imagine.

In my case, I felt deep loyalty to John Ehrlichman. My being in the White House was in part based on fifteen years of friendship between the Ehrlichman and Krogh families. The unquestioning zeal with which I approached the Pentagon Papers assignment—unquestioning not only about our mission but also about my ability to carry out the work—was rooted in the depth of the connection I had with Ehrlichman.

When my parents passed away in 1962, Ehrlichman became a surrogate father to me. Both Ehrlichman and Nixon would be strong male role models to me, and after my father's death when I was twenty-two, I was increasingly dependent on strong male role models for guidance. My father had been a giant in my life, a man of great accomplishment, wisdom, and grace. He died during the third month of my four-month Navy officer candidate school program. I had to make a decision during the weekend of his passing: whether to take emergency leave and go home for a period of time or to stay with my company where I was serving as assistant company commander, maintain the integrity of that command structure until we were commissioned, and complete my training. I asked myself what my dad would have wanted, and it was clear he would have desired that I finish the job at hand.

While I was in the Navy, Ehrlichman and I stayed in close touch, and he helped me get accepted to the University of Washington Law School in 1968. From my first year, I aspired to work in his Seattle law firm upon graduation; during school, I clerked for the firm and concentrated my studies and articles on land use and environmental law, the two areas in which Ehrlichman specialized.

Our families were very close. My wife Suzanne and I enjoyed many events with the Ehrlichmans: Christmas Eve parties, Thanksgiving Day touch football games, salmon bakes, and skiing trips. We even babysat for the five Ehrlichman children during an extended trip that John and his wife Jeanne took.

Ehrlichman's brilliance, command of the English language, and sense of humor were well known in Seattle and were on display as soon as he joined the staff. His early White House press briefing in which he described getting lost on a family vacation while navigating the maze of parkways across the Potomac between the Iwo Jima monument, the Pentagon, and Memorial Bridge was talked about for years in the press room. He had a sharp wit and a strong sense of the sardonic. Two phrases he coined, "It'll play in Peoria" and "Let him twist slowly, slowly in the wind," entered the American political lexicon as soon as they were uttered.

Ehrlichman also had an incredible memory. He once dazzled the Washington State Supreme Court when he brilliantly argued a complex land-use case on the morning after Nixon's plane had landed in Seattle for an overnight campaign stop. For the previous three months Ehrlichman had served the Nixon campaign as tour director, and he'd had no opportunity to review the briefs and documents during that time. The only preparation time he had was in the car with me as I drove him to Olympia, where he would argue the case. During his oral argument to the court, he was in total command of all of the relevant facts, the issues, and the points of law involved. As the junior associate on the case, I was simply awed by his performance. We found out later—a short time after we were working in the West Wing of the White House—that he had won the case by a close vote of five to four. I felt that it was Ehrlichman's brilliant advocacy that won the day.

Right after Nixon won the 1968 election on November 5, Ehrlichman met with the president-elect and senior campaign staff in California to determine how the transition office and the new White House would be staffed. The president-elect asked Ehrlichman to serve as counsel to the president. A few days later, Ehrlichman returned to Seattle to shut down his law practice and prepare for his move to the East Coast. The first day after his return from California, he came into my office, sat back in a chair, and put his feet up on my desk. "Do you like your work here?" he asked me with a mischievous smile.

"Yes, sir, I do," I answered.

"Would you consider changing it and coming to Washington, D.C., to serve as staff assistant to the counsel to the president?" he asked, raising his left eyebrow as he said it.

My answer was immediate: "Yes, sir, I certainly would!" I felt overwhelmed and elated at the opportunity he was giving me.

While he was intensely competitive and hated to lose in lawsuits or in games, he also possessed a great heart and could be counted on to help family and friends when the chips were down. Years later, when I told him about my impending divorce, he burst into tears of sympathy.

This was the Ehrlichman who took me aside in San Clemente: a family friend, a father figure, a brilliant mentor, an employer, and the principal person to whom I owed complete personal loyalty on the Nixon staff. As we finished our meeting that afternoon on July 17, Ehrlichman said that the president had expressly ordered that, before starting any work on this assignment, I was to read the chapter on the Hiss case in Nixon's book *Six Crises*. Ehrlichman stressed that it was important to infer from *Six Crises* what the president thought was at stake with Ellsberg's release of the Pentagon Papers and how the investigation should be approached.

That evening of July 17, I went back to my room at the Newporter Inn, twenty miles north of the western White House, where a number of staff members were staying while the president was in residence at San Clemente. I ordered dinner and sat down to reread the copy of *Six Crises* from Ehrlichman.

I had read *Six Crises* a few years earlier, soon after its publication, to get a better understanding of Nixon because Ehrlichman had worked for him as an advance man in the 1960 presidential campaign and later as tour director for Nixon's 1962 campaign for governor of California. While visiting Ehrlichman at the 1962 campaign headquarters on Wilshire Boulevard in Los Angeles, I was captivated by the mechanics of running a campaign and wished I could participate. But as a recently commissioned naval officer stationed on the USS *Yorktown*, an antisubmarine warfare aircraft carrier, I wasn't in a position in June 1962 to offer my services to the campaign.

When I first read *Six Crises*, I was impressed not only with the way Nixon worked through extremely demanding challenges, but also with the quality of his writing. But this time, I read it differently: now it was an assignment from the author—as president—to delve into one chapter, to glean the substantive ideas, and to learn how he wanted us to approach a major national security investigation.

Why did Nixon direct me to read the chapter on Alger Hiss before starting the investigation? First, I think by asking me to read about this high-ranking State Department official accused of being a communist spy for the Soviet Union, Nixon wanted me to understand unequivocally that he viewed the problems with Ellsberg's release of the Pentagon Papers as a full national security crisis, one comparable to the career-defining—for him—conviction of a traitor in the full glare of publicity in 1948. Nixon was offering me the chance to succeed as he had succeeded and to draw the obvious inference about what such a success might portend for my own future career in government.

Nixon was sure that Ellsberg had not functioned alone and that there were other conspirators who must have helped to get the Pentagon Papers out into the public domain. The president felt that their purpose was clearly to undermine his policies for ending the Vietnam War. (Much later, in 2004, Daniel Ellsberg confirmed to me that if he'd had access to Nixon's Vietnam War plans in 1971, he would certainly have released them to the press. He felt that Nixon was more committed to winning the Vietnam War than ending it.)

As I read the Hiss chapter, I tried hard to understand who Hiss really was and how he was relevant to the Ellsberg case. Alger Hiss was a senior official in the State Department who had participated in some of the most significant foreign policy events in the 1940s. He was present at Yalta with Roosevelt, Churchill, and Stalin. He was a well-established and respected member of the foreign policy elite, with impeccable academic credentials. And he was a Russian spy.

I learned about the key role played by Whittaker Chambers in uncovering the truth about Hiss. Chambers, a self-professed former communist, disclosed under oath to the House Committee on Un-American Activities that he knew Hiss well because they were both members of a Soviet spy ring operating in the United States. When Hiss was questioned under oath about whether he knew Chambers, he said he didn't know a man with the name of Whittaker Chambers. He was emphatic before Congress and elsewhere that he didn't know Chambers. After a period of intense questioning by the committee between August and December 1948, it was clear that Hiss was lying. Eventually convicted of perjury by the Department of Justice, he served a forty-four-month prison sentence. Nixon, by his own account in *Six Crises,* worked relentlessly on the case and frequently put in eighteen-hour days to put Hiss away.

The first and most basic impression I got from rereading the Hiss chapter was that Nixon viewed the uncovering of the truth about Hiss as vital to the national security. He wrote on page 10 of *Six Crises* that the House Committee on Un-American Activities, on which he served, "had an obligation running to the very security of the nation to dig out the truth." On page 40 he added: "But this case involved far more than the personal fortunes of Hiss, Chambers, myself, or the members of the Committee. *It involved the security of the whole nation and the cause of free men everywhere*" (emphasis added). It was a heroic endeavor, evidently, deeply connected to preserving American freedoms. What cause could be nobler? In reading the stirring sentences, I realized that he saw a parallel in Ellsberg's leak of the Pentagon Papers, but I overlooked one point: in both cases, there was no doubt in Nixon's mind that the man in question was a traitor long before there was any actual proof.

Although I did not recall it that evening, the year before, on August 3, 1970, President Nixon had publicly proclaimed guilt before actual evidence was presented. When Charles Manson went to trial, he had told the press right at the start that here was a man "who was guilty, directly or indirectly, of eight murders without reason." Because Manson was on trial and not convicted, the president's statement was fiercely criticized. Outrage came from many quarters, condemning the president for asserting guilt before trial in a country where a person is presumed innocent until proven guilty.

I learned about Nixon's Manson comment later that same day at the beginning of a major meeting I was running in Denver for the president and law enforcement officials from all fifty states. The purpose of the meeting was to emphasize the administration's new major financial support for state and local law enforcement. Ron Ziegler, the White House press secretary, came up to me before I opened the session and whispered, "It doesn't matter what you do in this meeting. No one will know. The president just told the world that Manson is guilty. We're going to be putting this fire out for the next few hours." I was deeply disappointed because of the time and effort so many people had put into the advance planning and management of the meeting.

While returning to the capital on *Air Force One* with the president, Ehrlichman, Ziegler, and I drafted a White House press release explaining that the president did not mean to assert guilt but that he was referring to allegations, and that the presumption of innocence was bedrock law in our country. We hadn't finished the press release by the time the plane was approaching Andrews Air Force Base, so we delayed landing, boring circular holes in the sky until we finally had a release acceptable to the staff and the president. After *Air Force One* landed, the press plane touched down, and we handed the release out to the press as they trooped off.

While reading *Six Crises* that evening of July 17, I did not discern the propensity of the president to rush to judgment without proof in the Manson case and his judgment before trial that Ellsberg was a traitor. I simply accepted the president's opinion.

On page 67 of *Six Crises* Nixon wrote: "As Herbert

Hoover wrote me after Hiss' conviction, 'at last the stream of treason that has existed in our government has been exposed in a fashion all may believe.' . . . The Hiss case aroused the nation for the first time to the existence and character of the Communist conspiracy within the United States."

The real meaning I was supposed to derive from reading the chapter on Hiss was that Hiss had conspirators in the spy ring, that it really was a national security crisis, and that Nixon had pulled out all the stops to put an end to Hiss's career as a spy. It was clear that Nixon hoped I would use a no less aggressive and intense approach in pursuit of Ellsberg, who to Nixon was clearly a traitor on the scale of Hiss and no doubt working with others to undermine the security of the United States. I finished reading very late that night. The next day, July 18, I reread some of the pertinent sections, reviewed the contents of the bucket file Ehrlichman had given me, and, with the president and staff, returned to Washington on *Air Force One*.

After reading the chapter and absorbing the lessons, I felt overwhelmed by the expectation that was being placed on me. I knew I had to commit a huge amount of time to establishing a new organization to direct the international narcotics control program, and I didn't know where I would find the time to do the Pentagon Papers job correctly. Someone with fewer other direct responsibilities would have to run day-to-day operations. We also needed help from an experienced investigator. As I prepared for the new work, I read that the Pentagon Papers described the errors in the Vietnam and Indochina policies of presidents before Nixon took office in 1968. Nothing in the papers related to Nixon's policies. But I still didn't question the reasons why Nixon was so driven to investigate Ellsberg.

In reflecting from the vantage point of today on what the president really wanted from the investigation and why I was given the assignment, I have been able to gain a great deal of insight from the transcripts of taped conversations of two other meetings in the Oval Office two weeks before my fateful meeting with Ehrlichman on July 17.

Both meetings were held on July 1, 1971, the first from 8:45 A.M. to 9:52 A.M. with the president, Haldeman, and Kissinger in attendance, and the second from 10:28 A.M. to 11:49 A.M. with the president, Haldeman, Colson, and Ehrlichman. Both meetings were tape recorded and have been reprinted in *Abuse of Power: The New Nixon Tapes.*

In the first meeting, during discussions about the Pentagon Papers, the president said:

> This is what I want. I have a project that I want somebody to take it just like I took the Hiss case. . . . And I'll tell you what. This takes—this takes eighteen hours a day. It takes devotion and dedication and loyalty and diligence such as you've never seen, Bob. I've never worked as hard in my life and I'll never work

as hard again because I don't have the energy for it. But this thing is a hell of a great opportunity because here is what it is.

In the second meeting that morning, the president discussed with Haldeman, Colson, and Ehrlichman the Supreme Court's ruling against the government on June 30, 1971. The administration had attempted to prevent *The New York Times* from publishing the Pentagon Papers and had been rebuffed. Nixon's bitterness about the decision was obvious. In the transcript of that meeting, Nixon said, "We're through with this sort of court case. . . . Go back and read the chapter on the Hiss case in *Six Crises* and you'll see how it was done. It wasn't done waiting for the goddamn courts or the attorney general or the FBI. . . . We have got to get going here."

In the most relevant section, which relates directly to their decision to pick me for the job, the president said:

Now do you see what we need? I really need a son of a bitch . . . who will work his butt off and do it dishonorably. Do you see what I mean? Who will know what he's doing and I want to know too. And I'll direct him myself. I know how to play this game and we're going to start playing it.

I can't have a high-minded lawyer like John Ehrlichman, or you know, Dean or somebody like that. I want somebody just as tough as I am for a change.

These kids don't understand, they have no understanding of politics, no understanding of public
relations. John Mitchell is that way, John is always
worried about is it technically correct. Do you think,
for chrissake, that the *New York Times* is worried
about all the legal niceties? Those sons of bitches are
killing me. I mean, thank god I leaked to the press
during the Hiss controversy. This is what we've got
to get. I want you to shake these [unintelligible] up
around here. Now you do it. Shake them up. Get
them off their goddamn dead asses, we're up against
an enemy, a conspiracy. They're using any means.
We are going to use any means. Is that clear?

Did they get the Brookings Institution raided last
night? No? Get it done. I want it done. I want the
Brookings Institution's safe cleaned out, and have it
cleaned out in a way that it makes somebody else
[responsible].

So why did I get the assignment? I speculate that I can
hardly have been the first choice. Nixon had wanted a
black-ops kind of guy, a "real son of a bitch." While I can't
confirm the president's exact feelings about my character
at the time, I don't think he viewed me as a "real son of
a bitch." I was the very thing he said he didn't want, a
"kid," and quite interested in the "technically correct"
myself. At the time my ironic nickname from colleagues
was "Evil" Krogh; I had a reputation as a somewhat rigid

moral do-gooder. Others were far more obvious candidates to run the investigation, none more so than Colson. I have always been curious why Colson wasn't given the principal responsibility for the Special Investigations Unit. He came to the White House with a reputation as a can-do kind of guy. He was willing to play political hardball. He even had a cartoon on his office wall showing a Vietnamese peasant with somebody's hand holding his testicles. Caption: "When you've got 'em by the balls their hearts and minds will follow."

So why wasn't Colson given the assignment of heading up the SIU? It may be that Ehrlichman and Haldeman were afraid of him. They were concerned that because Colson had a direct line to the president and was known to appeal to Nixon's darker side of paranoia and anger—his dark angels—that he would do things that would be dangerous and risky to the White House and the president. It was, of course, ironic that I—"Evil" Krogh—would conduct dangerous and risky activities despite a dearth of direct experience in black bag operations or direct access to the president and his dark side.

Another possible candidate for the Pentagon Papers job was John Dean, counsel to the president. But I learned much later that Dean—to his great credit—had single-handedly prevented the Brookings Institution raid from going forward as the president had expressly ordered on July 1, 1971. When Dean learned about the planned raid, he immediately flew to California and persuaded Ehrlichman to call it off. As a result of this courageous act, Dean was then viewed by Ehrlichman, Colson, and Haldeman as not aggressive enough to carry out the president's wishes in this case. Dean told me later that the reason he was not selected for the SIU was that he was viewed as a "little old lady" by the senior staff. We all would have been better off with Dean's "little old lady" perspective.

I learned much later, too, that Pat Buchanan, one of the president's favorite speechwriters, had turned down the assignment. He felt that it was more of an operational responsibility than a task for a White House policymaker and writer.

I guess I was chosen because I was the White House liaison with the FBI and with the Department of Justice. I was often assigned to resolve challenging problems for the administration, such as crime in the District of Columbia, our responses to antiwar protests, and the narcotics control programs. I was interested in the operational aspects of problem-solving. Even though I don't think I fit the dark profile the president wanted for the job, perhaps a simpler reason I got it was that it was understood that I would do it to the best of my ability and not ask questions. At that point in my White House career, I wasn't given to lengthy reflection on whether I was competent or experienced enough to do the jobs assigned to me. I certainly wasn't in the habit of questioning the orders or wisdom of my superiors, Ehrlichman and Nixon, to whom I gave complete loyalty. And I suppose that I did fit the other criteria the president spoke of on July 1; I was diligent, dedicated, and devoted to him.

So I accepted the task, and despite my other responsibilities, I set about making the time to manage a team that would have the highest priority to solve what I believed was a real national security problem. The Special Investigations Unit was a unit in name only. My first priority was to equip it with a discreet base. Then I had to find the plumbers.

2

THE PLUMBERS GATHER IN ROOM 16

On July 19, the day after my return to Washington, D.C., I debriefed members of my staff on my trip around the world on narcotics control issues. In addition to the follow-up work for the military drug program in South Vietnam, the president had directed us to move forward aggressively on forming the Cabinet Committee for International Narcotics Control. By bringing together the lead agencies with foreign responsibilities under the chairmanship of the secretary of state, William Rogers, we felt that we would have an effective organization to design and implement strong drug interdiction policies around the world. I was designated to serve as Secretary Rogers's executive director of the cabinet committee. Turning to the special investigations work right after these briefings,

I called G. Gordon Liddy and set up an appointment with him for the following day. Because of his previous experience as an FBI agent, prosecutor, and Republican loyalist, Liddy had received an appointment as special assistant to the secretary in the Treasury Department's law enforcement section. Gerald Ford, GOP minority leader in the House, had helped Liddy join the administration in March 1969, six weeks after President Nixon's inauguration.

Liddy had worked with me on numerous projects dealing with the narcotics interdiction programs under the Customs Service and gun control issues under the Bureau of Alcohol, Tobacco, and Firearms. A passionate gun enthusiast and loyal member of the National Rifle Association, Liddy argued aggressively and effectively in policy discussions against some of the more restrictive gun control initiatives that circulated in the administration. After he joined the SIU, I learned that during one of his legal arguments in a crowded courtroom Liddy had discharged a pistol to make a point. This apparently scared the wits out of those present and incurred a quick censure from the judge.

Liddy was also a friend of one of my best friends in the Justice Department, Donald Santarelli, who was serving as the associate deputy attorney general for policy. Santarelli, like Liddy, held strong conservative views, and both men advocated for muscular law enforcement tactics in the president's wars on crime and drugs. Santarelli had told me on several occasions how difficult a time Liddy was having at Treasury because of his numerous run-ins and conflicts with Gene Rossides, the assistant secretary of the Treasury for law enforcement. He suggested that if it were possible to find another position for Liddy in the administration, this move would be good for Liddy as well as for the policies we wanted to push forward.

Attorney General John Mitchell agreed with Santarelli that it would be a good move if Liddy could be brought to the White House. In a memo dated June 15, 1971, Santarelli confirmed that the attorney general was committed to finding a spot for Liddy on the White House staff. In an assignment that would surprise no one today, his areas of concentration would be narcotics and guns.

To do my job well, I felt it was critical to maintain a good professional and personal relationship with Attorney General Mitchell. In late November 1968, during the transition period from President Lyndon Johnson to President-elect Nixon, I had my first meeting with Mitchell at the offices of Nixon, Mudge, Rose, Guthrie & Alexander. This was the law firm where Mitchell and Nixon had worked as partners and where Mitchell had presided as Nixon's manager for the 1968 campaign. Mitchell was brusque, laconic, and somewhat sour when we first met and kept puffing on his pipe while we discussed several issues. But we became friends and stayed friendly over the next two years.

In July 1971, Mitchell had close and easy access to the president, so as the president's liaison with the Justice Department, I wanted to stay in Mitchell's good graces as much as I could. Hiring Liddy would help on all fronts.

On several occasions when I called Mitchell in the evening, I ended up talking with his wife, Martha, a loquacious Southern belle who had long blond hair and a vivacious smile and who tried to look younger than her years. She was also known for her uninhibited social behavior and inability to keep her personal views about the president and administration members to herself. Even though she became known as "the voice that launched a thousand quips," Mitchell adored her. At one of the first inaugural balls in 1969, I had found myself standing next to Mitchell. Martha was dancing with wild abandon with one of the ubiquitous military aides. Mitchell followed her every move like a cat. "Isn't she beautiful??!!" he said to me. "Absolutely beautiful, Mr. Mitchell, really, really stunning," I replied.

As a result of Santarelli's and Mitchell's efforts and my own need for another staff person who could help with my narcotics and law enforcement responsibilities, Liddy officially joined the White House staff on July 20, 1971. All of the paperwork had been done and the transfer from Treasury completed when he came over to my office, room 172, in the Old Executive Office Building (known to everyone as the "EOB").

Room 172 and a set of suites across the hall, plus a

few more offices down the center hall of the second floor of the EOB, were allocated to me and my staff when I was promoted to deputy assistant to the president for domestic affairs in early 1970. My office was painted yellow, with a very high ceiling, deep, plush, dark-blue carpeting, and elegant furniture in the Williamsburg style. Through the windows and from my porch, there was an extraordinary view of the White House and the north lawn where reporters then and today give their nightly news reports. The space was located three offices north of Nixon's hideaway office, which he frequently occupied when he needed to get away from the constant interactions in the West Wing and the Oval Office.

Office location in the Nixon White House reflected in large degree the status of the staff member and was controlled with Prussian precision by Haldeman, the chief of staff. The most senior positions—the chief of staff, the national security adviser, the head of congressional relations, various cabinet-level counselors to the president, and their immediate staffs—all had offices in the West Wing.

My first job on the staff was as staff assistant to the counsel to the president. John Ehrlichman was counsel to the president, so my office was a tiny alcove across from his much larger wood-paneled office on the second floor of the West Wing. To help compensate for my lack of experience, Jana Hruska, Ehrlichman's secretary and daughter of Nebraska senator Roman Hruska, took on the job of educating me in the ways of Washington. She knew everyone of importance in the capital and kept me from making bonehead blunders in protocol and professional courtesies. "Yes, Bud," she would admonish, "you *do* call a senator back within an hour of his call. A congressman can wait a couple of hours. You must always take a cabinet secretary's call immediately. And your wife's!"

Ehrlichman's office was directly above the Oval Office. Quite frequently when I was in visiting him, he would get buzzed on his phone from the line that was identified as POTUS, for "President of the United States." Ehrlichman would pick up the phone, hit the POTUS button, and discuss some matter briefly, often with a "Yes, Mr. President," or "No, Mr. President." If he said "Yes, sir, I'll be right there," he'd hang up and say something like, "OK, down the flag pole to the leader of the Western World," and rush out the door.

I sized up my new staff member when Liddy walked into room 172. He was about five-foot-ten, two inches shorter than me, and carried himself with ramrod-erect posture. A dark-complexioned man, he had thinning brown hair and heavy eyebrows over piercing dark eyes. He sported a bushy moustache and moved with a forceful, purposeful energy. When we shook hands, his grip was vise-like.

I formally welcomed him to the White House and my staff and expressed some regret that I had been unable to get him on board sooner. However, when Rossides and his colleague at the Treasury Department, Charles Walker, the deputy secretary, had heard about Liddy's transfer to the White House, they were extremely angry. They told me they feared Liddy would undermine their policy advice to the president on gun control issues and insisted that Liddy have no policy responsibility for gun control policy while serving on my staff. Their position was way beyond their prerogative once he worked for me. We worked out a way for Liddy to continue to work on gun control matters by advising Geoffrey Shepard, another staff member of mine, who had direct responsibility for gun control policy.

Liddy said he understood how difficult it was to get the transfer done but was just glad to be there. Liddy was the kind of guy you'd want next to you in a foxhole, where he'd cover your back and take a bullet to save your life. He projected a warrior-type charisma and seemed to possess a great deal of physical courage. He was tough, smart, disciplined, and loyal. In the following years during the Watergate investigations Liddy never "squealed" or "snitched" on anyone.

But there was also a strain of fanaticism in Liddy's character that I did not fully appreciate in the early weeks of our work together. His silence and conviction to stay true to his own personal code of honor long after others had sold out prompted me once to liken him to Lieutenant Hiroo Onoda, the Japanese officer who refused to surrender and fought his own personal war in the Philippines for twenty-nine years after the surrender by the Japanese empire in 1945.

I told Liddy that since we had first started talking about his joining my staff to work on narcotics, bombing, and guns, another project had come up. The project, which was related directly to national security, was of utmost gravity and importance to the president. I told him it would require all of his background and skill as a former FBI special agent and would involve the most intense effort over the next several weeks. He told me he was there to serve the president, and me, in any way he could, and that he would be honored to take on a crucial national security project.

With his consent to work on the project, I took Liddy over to meet Young. Young had already been assigned to the SIU from Kissinger's staff while I was in San Clemente. Because there was so much urgency to get underway, Young had arranged to use a temporary office near mine until another secure office location could be found elsewhere in the EOB.

When I brought Liddy in to meet Young, Young stood up and shook Liddy's hand. While I knew both men were accomplished lawyers and had graduated from excellent law schools—Young from Cornell and Liddy from Fordham—I could immediately see some stark differences between them in personal appearance and mannerisms. Where Liddy was dark, forceful, and packed with intense emotional energy, Young was light-complexioned, laid-back, and somewhat professorial in his demeanor. With thinning blond hair and light-blue eyes set in a narrow face, Young smiled a lot and spoke in whispered tones. He looked like a quintessential Englishman, the kind of man depicted in World War II films who flew fighters for the Royal Air Force during the 1940 Blitz bombing of London and who would always understate the dangers he faced. I felt that the skills of each man as I knew them would be used to the maximum over the weeks ahead.

We talked briefly about the nature of the project—to investigate all aspects of the Pentagon Papers release to the press—but we did not get into any depth that first day. We did discuss the reporting arrangements. Although Young came from Kissinger's staff, all information developed by the unit would be routed to Ehrlichman and not Kissinger—an arrangement Ehrlichman had established in San Clemente. As far as I was aware, Kissinger was not informed by Young about any of the investigative work of the Plumbers. Ehrlichman was responsible for what was communicated to the president. I told them I had not been instructed personally by the president but had received all of my direction from Ehrlichman in San Clemente. I told them I had not been relieved of my primary duties on narcotics control, and in particular that I would be extremely busy over the next few weeks in setting up the Cabinet Committee for International Narcotics Control.

Young confirmed that he would be working with the unit full-time, and that, as the on-site codirector of the unit, he would have primary responsibility for the day-to-day, even hour-by-hour, flow of information by memo and phone call. Young also said he would take the responsibility for drafting the memos generated by the unit unless Liddy was given a specific written assignment. Liddy was asked later to prepare a memorandum on the less-than-satisfactory support and backup from the FBI during the subsequent work of the unit. His memorandum received wide circulation in the White House, up to and including the president.

Liddy accepted this administrative setup, which required him to take direction from both Young and myself on the work of the SIU. I also made clear that on any other assignments related to narcotics or gun control, Liddy worked for me.

Now it was time to find a secure home for the SIU. Room 16 was located at the far southwest corner on the first floor of the EOB. When I first explored the former mail room area where the SIU would be located, I thought it would be too exposed for the kind of ultra-sensitive secret work we would be doing, but in fact, the space proved secure partly because by its very ordinariness it managed to hide itself in plain sight. Staff members and support people who worked in offices along the south and west corridors of the EOB would frequently walk right by room 16. Heavy bars covered the thick glass in the windows that looked out on Seventeenth Street to the west and to the adjacent park and Ellipse to the south. Only the designation ROOM 16 was visible on the high, nondescript, dark-paneled door. Even though there was some exposure to regular foot traffic, it was still apart from the regularly traveled corridors, and so I was able to get from my main office to room 16 quickly and without drawing much attention to where I was going. It took about three days to get the space up and running.

Toward the end of our first week, E. Howard Hunt came to the unit and introduced himself to me and Young. He said that Colson had assigned him to work with the unit, and that Colson would be interested in any information uncovered during the investigation of Ellsberg. Ehrlichman told me that Hunt, not I, would be the channel to Colson for this information. Colson was to be in charge of communicating information to the media and Congress.

A short, dapper man, Hunt had a sharp, aquiline nose, light features, sandy hair, and a ready smile. He told us he'd had a long career with the CIA, had run agents primarily in Latin America, and was involved in the Bay of Pigs invasion in 1961. I immediately wanted to know a whole lot more about his involvement. The Bay of Pigs had, after all, been nothing short of a foreign policy disaster for the Kennedy administration. I learned later that Hunt believed President Kennedy had made some bad decisions in the Bay of Pigs crisis that resulted in the deaths of many of his former colleagues in the anti-Castro Cuban community. He said that while he was not officially working for "the Agency" any longer, he had maintained good contacts there that could be useful to us.

During this first meeting with Hunt, I was struck by how unassuming, retiring, and diffident he seemed. He could blend easily into any group without drawing undue attention, a valuable characteristic for a spy.

Hunt felt that it would be helpful for him to have a special, secure phone for his personal use. Kathy Chenow, the secretary brought to work for the unit, set up this phone with all bills to be sent to her home address—a highly unusual arrangement in traditional government work. In addition to Hunt's special phone, a "scrambler" telephone system was also set up to ensure that our calls could not be overheard or monitored by anyone. Others in the unit had far more experience in matters of subterfuge than I had. For me, the combined elements of secrecy—the scrambler, the hidden office, the security systems—were clear warnings of the dark waters we were wading into.

When we were set up with office equipment, Young moved into the principal suboffice behind Chenow's desk, with windows facing Seventeenth Street and East Executive Drive. A large conference table was set up in the center suboffice, and it was here that we held our first meeting as a team on July 23. It had taken less than a week to assemble the team and the facilities that would become known as "the Plumbers" later in 1971 over Thanksgiving. The staff was complete: we were Bud Krogh, Gordon Liddy, E. Howard Hunt, David Young, and Kathy Chenow.

At the beginning of our first meeting together, we discussed how Ehrlichman had described the assignment. I emphasized that the president viewed our work as critical to America's national security, and that we would be operating with full support from senior staff and from the president. The president's sense of urgency, so clearly communicated in his assignment of *Six Crises,* permeated the room. We were a new team, rushing to execute a top secret and critically important mission ordered by the commander in chief, and we could each feel the weight of the assignment.

We were to leave no stone unturned in our investigation of the leak of the top secret Pentagon Papers to *The New York Times.* Specifically, we needed to determine Ellsberg's reason for releasing the papers and the identity of his collaborators. Had he leaked these documents alone or was he part of a conspiracy? We needed to assess the likelihood that he had access to other top secret information related to President Nixon's plans for ending the Vietnam War, and if so, determine whether he would be likely to leak this information as well.

One of the unit's first acts was to request any "damage assessments" from the CIA and the FBI that they might have prepared about the disclosure of the Pentagon Papers. These assessments would give the unit some understanding of the impacts of the leak on U.S. intelligence systems, methods, and operations. In response to this request, the CIA provided a damage assessment it had prepared before the SIU was set up.

The CIA's assessment reported grounds to believe that

a full set of the Pentagon Papers had reached the Soviet embassy in D.C., before *The New York Times* started publishing its versions on June 13, 1971. Right after the SIU was set up, the FBI provided corroborating intelligence that a full set of the Pentagon Papers had indeed reached the Soviet embassy ahead of publication in the *Times*. We knew, however, that the *Times* had received only a partial set of the Pentagon Papers. This intelligence, raw and unconfirmed though it was, heightened our suspicions that Ellsberg or one of his collaborators, if he had any, may have had some sort of foreign involvement.

Hunt told us that from this damage assessment and other information he had seen to date, it was not unlikely that Ellsberg had some type of Soviet involvement. The Soviet Union was a major supplier of war materiel to the North Vietnamese. Soviet-built radar systems tracked American planes, Soviet surface-to-air missiles shot them down, and the AK-47 was the rifle used by the Viet Cong and the North Vietnamese Army to kill American soldiers. It was not a stretch of logic to assume that the Soviet Union would support public release of the Pentagon Papers to rally more public opinion in opposition to the Vietnam War. Moreover, Hunt suggested that any information linking Ellsberg with the Soviets, either directly or indirectly, could be used to discredit Ellsberg and thus undermine any credibility he might have in the public arena.

After our first meeting, a mood of manic resolve to carry out our duties drove us forward. The unit had been given a critical responsibility by the president, and we were embarking on a quest that held great import for the security of the nation. I was confident that we all agreed that Ellsberg was very likely at the center of a Soviet-sponsored conspiracy to diminish U.S. influence in the critical theater of Vietnam. It was an easy conclusion to reach, somehow made all the easier by the complete lack of corroborating evidence. Any doubts we might have nurtured were quickly dispelled; indeed, the unit's high level of resolve and spirit of urgency were vastly increased by the next leak of top secret information, which was the subject of my meeting with the president and Ehrlichman in the Oval Office on July 24, 1971.

3

A NEW LEAK FOR THE PLUMBERS

On Saturday, July 24, 1971, around 10:00 A.M., Ehrlichman called and told me to drop whatever I was doing and meet him outside the Oval Office. The president wanted to see us immediately. A story by William Beecher had just run the day before in *The New York Times* that revealed the fallback position of the United States in the first Strategic Arms Limitation Talks (SALT I) in Helsinki. Ehrlichman said the president was very, very angry.

Since publication of the story, I had been in regular contact with Al Haig, the deputy national security adviser, regarding who might have leaked the top secret information to Beecher. Haig told me he had received some initial information from his contacts at the Department of Defense on possible suspects who had access to the information and who might have been in touch with Beecher. He said that officials in the DOD general counsel's office were investigating and following up on every lead. I learned later that Haig had shared this same information with Ehrlichman.

The headline of the Beecher story was "U.S. Urges Soviet to Join in a Missiles Moratorium," and the subheadline was, "Would Halt Construction of Land and Sea Arms and Allow Each Nation Up to 300 Antimissile Weapons." The story detailed the elements of proposals that were being considered by the U.S. side for presentation at the SALT I talks between the Soviet Union and the United States. The story set out some "ambitious proposals" that the U.S. negotiators were considering privately but had not yet been developed into specific draft language to present to the Soviets. It also contained specific information from the still secret American proposals regarding the choice each nation could make "between defending its capital with 100 antiballistic missiles or employing up to 300 defensive missiles, at three sites, to defend offensive missiles."

I had read the Beecher article carefully, but I wasn't familiar with the components of the American proposal, and I was not at all informed about the complex and murky arcana of the technical aspects of the SALT I talks. Leadership for determining the U.S. positions was assigned to Kissinger and the National Security Council, with technical support from the DOD and the Arms Control and Disarmament Agency. Specifically, Kissinger provided policy guidance to Gerard Smith, the ACDA director and the principal negotiator for the United States in Helsinki. I was well aware—as I believe were most White House staff members—that success in the SALT I negotiations with the Soviets was considered by the president and Kissinger one of the most critical foreign policy objectives and national security programs that the Nixon administration had launched. On the same day President Nixon was inaugurated, January 20, 1969, the Soviet Foreign Ministry had indicated its interest in pursuing strategic arms limitation discussions with the United States. The president indicated his support for the talks immediately thereafter.

The survival of the planet was potentially at stake in the effort to control the increase of nuclear weapons on the part of both the United States and the Soviet Union. A deal with the Soviets where both sides implicitly rejected the idea of using nuclear weapons and reduced their nuclear arsenals was to me the ultimate national security imperative.

In 1971 the Soviet Union was still a formidable power, and the Cold War was still cold. Even though the SALT I talks reflected a gradual thawing, the United States was still engaged in high-stakes military competition with the Soviet Union. Each country possessed sufficient nuclear weapons to annihilate the other. Mutual assured destruction, appropriately known as MAD, was the Armageddon prospect that kept each country from risking its own self-destruction. The purpose of SALT I was to reduce the number of nuclear weapons each side could have so that the risk of nuclear war could be correspondingly reduced.

I had realized on first reading the Beecher article that a leak of this kind was obviously going to be of great concern to the president, and I was right.

After Ehrlichman rang off, I grabbed my yellow pad, rushed out of my office, and speed-walked across West Executive Drive to the West Wing. When I arrived at the secretary's desk outside the Oval Office, Ehrlichman was already there. After waiting only a few seconds, the secretary told us to go in.

I followed Ehrlichman into the Oval Office. As we approached the president's desk, I felt the chill and tightening in my gut that I always felt when going into a meeting with him. Each president redecorates the Oval Office according to his taste, and I always found Nixon's Oval Office stark, cold, and austere. To the right of his massive desk, five service flags stood sentinel, each flag topped by a golden eagle. A black phone sat on the left side of the president's desk. Two chairs upholstered in gold abutted the desk on the right and left side. A collection of ceramic birds was perched on wall shelves on either side of the door to the president's private office. Other than the presidential seal that hung on the wall just to the left of the door to the Secret Service agent's station—the seal had been embroidered by Julie Nixon Eisenhower during the campaign and given to her father when he had "gone over the top" to win the 1968 election—there wasn't a square centimeter of space in the Oval Office that was warm, intimate, or inviting. A large, oval, blue rug ringed with gold stars covered the floor. An eagle was woven into the center of the blue rug, and another was emblazoned in the plaster of the ceiling. Two couches faced each other antagonistically in front of an empty fireplace.

I realized later that Nixon's choices of trappings were designed in part to intimidate visitors, particularly those from other countries, with the power and majesty of his presidency. It was no wonder that the president had set up a much warmer and more comfortable private office in the EOB where he could relax, think, and write.

The president was pacing behind his desk, and his mood was obvious: he was extremely upset and very angry. His face was darkly flushed, and he didn't smile at either of us when we got close to his desk. According to the transcript of this meeting, there was an "inaudible section" when it started. This was when the president was still pacing and Ehrlichman and I had not yet sat down at our chairs by his desk. The president said he was not going to stand for Beecher-type leaks anymore. He slammed his right fist into his open left hand to emphasize his point. I told him we had some information about the potential leaker in the Department of Defense, and that we were considering administering a polygraph test to this suspect. The president then waved us to the chairs next to his desk (and thus within the reach of the bugs embedded in that desk), and our meeting continued.

After I told him about a suspect for the leak, the president said, "I think that's a place to start. Hook this guy. Hit it very hard, consider it [a] true fight." I mentioned possibly polygraphing this suspect, and the president said, "Take it over. And then immediately get a confession from him. Start with him."

Ehrlichman then cautioned the president that, in Haig's opinion, if we proceeded with the polygraphs and the pressure, we were sure to get resignations and legal action. We discussed polygraphing twenty or thirty people. While the transcript indicates that either Ehrlichman or I said, "Fine. Start there and let's screw the hell out of that guy and the people around him in that unit," in fact this was the president's comment. Ehrlichman then summarized the status of our investigation so far:

> Well, we've got one person, that comes out of DOD according to Al Haig, who is the prime suspect right now, a man by the name of Van Cleve who they feel is very much the guy that did it. Spent two hours with Beecher apparently this week, he had access to the documents. Uh, he apparently had views very similar to those which were reflected in the Beecher article, and it would be my feeling that we should begin with him, and go immediately around him before going to a dragnet polygraph of any other people.

After the president agreed that we should start with Van Cleve, Ehrlichman suggested that polygraphs should follow if Van Cleve turned out not to be the one. The president asked whether any of these potential leakers were more hawkish or dovish, to which Ehrlichman responded that Haig couldn't tell anything about that at this point. The president then said, "I don't care whether he's a hawk or a dove or anything. Now that the thing's leaked, he's up with the government."

The president then said, after probing whether a million people really had top secret clearances, "Here's what I want. . . . Little people do not leak. This crap . . . this crap is never-ending. I studied these cases long enough and it's always the son of a bitch that leaks."

"Ellsberg," I put in, nodding, and repeated, "Ellsberg!"

"Sure," the president responded, "so, what I would like to do is have everybody down through GS-something-or-other, you know, the Foreign Service . . . you know what I mean . . . ? Here in Washington I want all of them who have top secret clearances . . . to take part. And then I think maybe another approach would be to set up a . . . classification, alright, which we would call what?"

We brainstormed possible classifications that could protect the most sensitive information that the president deemed important. The president ruled out using "presidential" in any classification scheme, saying, "Don't use my . . . goddamn office." He then suggested a number of possibilities for the new classification scheme. He continued: "So we'll know what people had it. Now, the fact that a hundred had it. . . . I want to find out why a hundred had it."

Before I was assigned to codirect the SIU with Young on July 17, a program had launched within the national security apparatus of the government to declassify information that had no real justification for being classified. I learned that one of the principal reasons leaks of classified information occurred was due to the antiquated and unworkable classification system. So much information was classified that it was almost impossible to maintain the secrecy of the information that was truly sensitive and dangerous if disclosed. The president then told Ehrlichman and me that the declassification group should have been done with their work already. "Well, goddamn it, I told them two weeks ago . . . they should follow up on it. Nobody at all is up on a goddamned thing. We've got to follow up on this thing, however."

Ehrlichman answered, "They're going to come back at you with a whole new classification scheme."

The president shot back angrily, "But they didn't. But they didn't." Trying to respond to the president's dissatisfaction with the pace of the declassification work and to inject some realism into our discussion, I said quietly that it would take a while longer to develop a new classification scheme.

The president then circled back to polygraphing. He said we had to limit the number of people who had access to the most sensitive national security information. After searching again for a useful descriptor—"national security . . . with three letters like FM or SMS"—the president said that everyone who gets this information "must sign an agreement to take a polygraph. . . . [W]ith regard to the agreement to take a polygraph pledge: I want that to be done now, with about four or five hundred people in State, Defense . . . so that we can immediately enter that. Don't you figure that?"

"Yes, I do," answered Ehrlichman.

I then added, "Yes, sir, we're going to have drafts of that waiver prepared and stamps, we're going to have to look at what the stamps [of the new classification will state]."

The president then targeted the people and agencies to be covered by the new system: "The top executives of the government . . . that should include everybody on the NSC staff, for example. You start with them. You should include about a hundred people. . . . Probably four or five hundred at State, four or five hundred at Defense, and . . . two or three hundred over at . . . CIA . . . that's it. I don't care about these other agencies. All CIA people have gone through a polygraph."

After laying out his target groups, the president then said, "I don't know anything about polygraphs, and I don't know how accurate they are, but I know they'll scare the hell out of people."

I agreed with the president that polygraphs usually scared people because they ask a lot of personal questions. But I said that the upcoming polygraphs would focus much more specifically on a few questions about the Beecher story and contacts with him. Ehrlichman added that we would follow up on Haig's advice to focus on Van Cleve.

Ehrlichman then promised that we would work on it through the weekend and send anything we found on to the president. Nixon made it clear that he would be available, day or night.

Ehrlichman added, "Alright, I just wanted to know. And if we catch the guy, and his resignation is to be demanded . . ."

The president then hunched forward, sliced the air with his hand, and said angrily, "Not quiet. Alright, understand . . . You catch anybody, it's not going to be quiet, I'm gonna, we're gonna put the goddamn story out. He's going to be dismissed, prosecuted. . . ."

Ehrlichman cautioned again, "Uh, the polygraph is not useful for prosecution."

The president retorted, "Alright, but the point is that if a charge is made against him, that we're going to have to see that he's to be prosecuted. . . . I'll let you work the guy out."

The president then looked directly at me and said, "Alright?" I nodded. He then said, with his voice rising, "This does affect the national security, this is a case for measures . . . like the Pentagon Papers. This would involve the current negotiation, and it should not [be] getting out, jeopardizing . . . the negotiation position." He then pointed at me and almost shouted, "Now, goddamn it, we're not going to allow that. We're just not going to allow it." He then dismissed me with a wave and a cursory "Good luck."

Once the president rose from his chair and it was clear that he had concluded, Ehrlichman and I got up to leave. The president indicated that he wanted to talk with Ehrlichman alone as he headed toward the door leading out to the Rose Garden and to *Marine One,* the president's helicopter. It had been idling on the south lawn for most of our meeting, ready to take the him to Camp David.

As I walked out of the Oval Office, I felt an overwhelming sense of personal responsibility to take whatever action might be necessary to stop the kinds of leaks that were imperiling the president's negotiations. By directly connecting the Pentagon Papers and SALT I leaks to their effect on national security, Nixon made me feel even more that my assignment was of utmost importance. As I understood it, I was engaged in protecting two of the paramount national security objectives of the time: reducing the threat of nuclear war by a successful negotiation with the Soviet Union in the SALT I talks and minimizing the negative effect of the release of the Pentagon Papers on the president's policy for ending the Vietnam War.

At the time, I did not scrutinize the level of threat these two leaks posed to national security. The very words "national security" served to block critical analysis. The most basic definition of the term "national security" is the broad set of policies, programs, and activities that protect the survival of the nation. It seemed at the very least presumptuous, if not unpatriotic, for me to inquire into just what the significance to national security was in those two leaks. For me to suggest that national security was being improperly invoked would have been to invite a confrontation with both patriotism and loyalty. That kind of confrontation was well beyond what I was capable of at the time.

4

SPARRING WITH THE CIA, FBI, AND "DEEP THROAT"

Once out of the Oval Office, I rushed back to my office in the EOB, sat down, and called Liddy and Young. Liddy was in room 16 that Saturday morning, but Young was not. I took a circuitous route down two halls of the EOB and down one flight of stairs to room 16. Like other members of the unit, I tried to keep both the existence of room 16 and the fact that I worked there on occasion as confidential as I could. When I knocked on the door, Liddy opened it quickly. I walked in, asked him to join me in the conference room, and recounted what had just happened.

I gave him a detailed account of my meeting with the president and Ehrlichman and explained that the work of the unit had been officially expanded by the commander in chief to cover the SALT I leak of the day before. I stressed that I had never been in a meeting with the president where he was so incredibly angry.

When Liddy asked specifically how the president felt and what he had said, I answered that he looked flushed and very disturbed. The president had punched and sliced the air with his hands and fists, using several "goddamns" to emphasize his points. I told Liddy the president had placed the responsibility for not allowing any more of these leaks squarely on me and our team. His final order was that we were to go after the SALT I leak with the same no-holds-barred measures we were using in investigating Ellsberg and the leak of the Pentagon Papers. The SIU was now operating with a whole new sense of mission.

I needed to immediately arrange for the polygraphs that the president wanted, starting that day and continuing through the weekend. My first call was to the director of central intelligence (DCI), Richard Helms. In about five minutes, the White House operator located him on a tennis court. Like all DCIs, Helms was never more than a few minutes away from phone contact with his agency and the White House.

When he came on the line a little breathless, I explained to him that I had just come from a meeting with the president, who was furious about the leak of the SALT I fallback negotiating position in William Beecher's *New York Times* article the day before. I told him the president wasn't going to "allow" this to continue and that he had ordered us to conduct polygraph tests right away on officials who may have had access to our negotiating positions. I asked him if he could provide machines and operators to get started on these polygraph tests.

Helms quietly heard me out. He then told me in clear, unequivocal language that he had neither the polygraph machines nor the trained operators who could be pulled into service on such short notice. He explained that while the CIA regularly conducts polygraphs of their employees, these tests weren't something that could be pulled together quickly. While he was affable and sounded like he would like to help, Helms was nevertheless giving me a firm brush-off. Over-the-top demands from the Oval Office and hundreds of polygraphs administered over a few days was too implausible for Helms to take seriously.

Although I was disappointed in Helms's response, I wasn't surprised. As we had just advised the president, the information we had received to that point indicated that the likely source of the leak was a DOD official. Through his own intelligence, Helms may have already been aware of the same likelihood.

The relationship between DOD and the CIA, then as now, was often acrimonious and bitter. Helms may have been unwilling to exacerbate the interagency rivalry by lending CIA assets to a hunt for a DOD leaker, which DOD could have construed as an attack. I had been in meetings where representatives of DOD and the CIA disagreed with each other and where, like poised scorpions, they would circle each other waiting for an opportunity to strike. The relationship between the FBI and the CIA was even worse. They often wouldn't even talk to each other, let alone share intelligence. Or Helms may have just realized that a high-pressure request from an intense young White House aide on a Saturday morning wasn't the kind of careful, well-thought-through request that should be honored.

As part of my international narcotics control work, I had developed good working relationships with a few CIA officials and station chiefs in Burma and Laos, but I had not had regular dealings with Helms. My memory of Dick Helms is of a man of razor-sharp intelligence, patrician bearing, and a steely resolve to keep the Agency out of trouble in the internecine agency wars that were waged in the Nixon administration. He also would go to great lengths, including false declarations before Congress, to keep the secrets of the CIA. He was the consummate gentleman spy. So in spite of being disappointed to some degree in Helms's response, I didn't belabor it or indicate any dissatisfaction to him.

My next call was to the director of the Federal Bureau of Investigation, J. Edgar Hoover. It wasn't always easy to make contact with the director, even with a call from the White House on behalf of the president. One of my responsibilities was to act as liaison between the Bureau and the White House on law enforcement issues designated by Ehrlichman. I also dealt with policy issues, such as Bureau staffing at home and in U.S. embassies abroad and, specifically, how the federal government should respond to antiwar protests and civil disorders.

For the first few months of the Nixon administration, as staff assistant to the counsel to the president, I had also been entrusted with reading and evaluating all of the FBI full field investigation reports on nominees to key federal positions in the departments and agencies. Even though I was assigned to read these kinds of personal, sensitive documents, I was not in the loop on the more secret national security wiretaps that were requested from the FBI by Haldeman and Ehrlichman. Targets included the media and national security staff. These wiretap requests were usually made with the knowledge and endorsement of Dr. Kissinger and the president. I did know that Hoover had a direct communication link with the president, but I was not privy to either the substance or the frequency of those contacts. As a result of this compartmentalization of White House staff, no one had a complete, overall picture of the critical relationship between the Bureau and the White House. When I was asked to arrange a meeting for the president and Hoover, it was always necessary for me to get several open times on the president's schedule and offer them to the director so he could determine when it was convenient for him to come to the White House. In those days in the twilight of Hoover's career, it was commonly assumed that he had amassed a tremendous amount of confidential and potentially damaging information on practically everyone of consequence in the government. This knowledge instilled fear in many people. No one wanted to risk offending Hoover.

On that Saturday morning, July 24, I was successful in getting through to Hoover very quickly. As I had done with Helms, I explained what had just happened in my meeting with the president. Hoover listened carefully. He said he thought the Bureau might have a polygraph machine and an operator available. But under no circumstances could a test be done over the weekend. And he was talking about one test, not several, as the president had preferred.

I knew that it took time, sometimes days, to set up a polygraph test, to formulate the questions, and to prepare both the administrator and the test taker. I had just told the president that in any polygraph tests we initiated we would limit the questions to circumstances surrounding the SALT I leak, particularly the question of who had access to William Beecher and what was said between them. I repeated this to Hoover. He said he would work with us, and when I told him I was going to set up a meeting that afternoon to discuss how to proceed, he said he would send Mark Felt, the number three man in the Bureau, to attend the meeting. I thanked him and rang off.

Liddy had called Hunt and asked him to join us in room 16. I briefed Hunt on the events and calls of that morning and requested that he and Liddy join me in the meeting that afternoon to pursue the SALT I investigation further. I then called Bob Mardian, the assistant attorney general for internal security, and invited him to the meeting along with Mark Felt. I also invited J. Fred Buzhardt, the general counsel of the DOD, who had been assigned to investigate the DOD leak.

The meeting started early Saturday afternoon in the Roosevelt Room, a large, elegant meeting place directly across from the Oval Office in the West Wing. As associate director of the Domestic Council and deputy assistant to the president, I went to the Roosevelt Room weekday mornings at seven thirty when Congress was in session. These meetings were attended by my colleagues on the Domestic Council, senior staff from the Office of Management and Budget, and the White House congressional relations staff. Serious discussions on current policy issues occurred daily, and major decisions were made in the Roosevelt Room. The famous painting of Theodore Roosevelt leading the charge up San Juan Hill during the Spanish-American War hung on the north wall, enhancing the room's sense of history. I wanted to impress upon Mardian, Felt, and Buzhardt that the SALT I leak was a matter of utmost importance to the president. Meeting in the Roosevelt Room would underscore the gravity of the situation.

A description of this meeting in the Roosevelt Room was included in an article by John D. O'Connor in the July 2005 *Vanity Fair* article entitled "I'm the Guy They Called Deep Throat." O'Connor, who was at times a lawyer for Mark Felt's family, described Felt's account of this meeting:

Well before Hoover's death, relations between the Nixon camp and the F.B.I. deteriorated. In 1971, Felt was called to 1600 Pennsylvania Avenue. The President, Felt was told, had begun "climbing the walls" because someone (a government insider, Nixon believed) was leaking details to *The New York Times* about the administration's strategy for upcoming arms talks with the Soviets. Nixon's aides wanted the bureau to find the culprit, either through wiretaps or by insisting that suspects submit to lie-detector tests. Such leaks led the White House to begin employing ex-CIA types to do their own, homespun spying, creating its nefarious "Plumbers" unit, to which the Watergate cadre belonged.

Felt arrived at the White House to confront an odd gathering. Egil "Bud" Krogh, Jr., deputy assistant to the President for domestic affairs, presided, and attendees included ex-spy Hunt and Robert Mardian, an assistant Attorney General—"a balding little man," Felt recalled, "dressed in what looked like work clothes and dirty tennis shoes . . . shuffling about the room, arranging the chairs and I [first] took him to be a member of the cleaning staff." (Mardian had been summoned to the West Wing from a weekend tennis game.) According to Felt, once the meeting began, Felt expressed resistance to the idea of wiretapping suspected leakers without a court order.

After the session, which ended with no clear resolution, Krogh's group began to have reason to suspect a single Pentagon employee. Nixon, nonetheless, demanded that "four or five hundred people in State, Defense, and so forth [also be polygraphed] so that we can immediately scare the bastards." Two days later, as Felt wrote in his book, he was relieved when Krogh told him that the Administration had decided to let "the Agency," not the FBI, "handle the polygraph interviews. . . . Obviously, John Ehrlichman [Krogh's boss, Nixon's top domestic-policy adviser, and the head of the Plumbers unit] had decided to 'punish' the Bureau for what he saw as its lack of cooperation and its refusal to get involved in the work which the 'Plumbers' later undertook."

The real story was somewhat different. First, I thanked the men for coming to the White House on such short notice. All of them, unlike Liddy and me, were in their weekend clothes. I emphasized that the president wanted us to pursue an individual in the DOD as aggressively as we could over the weekend, and that this might require one or several lie-detector tests. I did not mention placing a wiretap without a warrant as part of the investigation. So there was no need for Felt to express "resistance to the idea of wiretapping suspected leakers without a court order." I stayed within the framework of pushing for fairly widespread polygraphs of leak suspects that I had just discussed two hours earlier with the president and Ehrlichman.

On July 24, I had not yet determined that the FBI was not committed to helping the SIU aggressively pursue leak investigations. That came later. So there was no pre-disposition on that day to be critical of the Bureau or to want to "punish" them two days later. It may well be that Felt lumped together some of his meetings later with junior White House staff members with this July 24 meeting on the SALT I leak. I had met with Felt on several occasions and always found him to be a very classy man, smart, competent, and ready to help. It seems odd that Felt would include this meeting as one in a series of meetings in which young White House staff members abused their authority or were trying to damage the Bureau, thus justifying his later decision to provide Watergate investigative material to Bob Woodward, who originated Felt's nickname "Deep Throat" for his colleagues on the *Washington Post* staff.

I did, however, repeat some of the president's strong language about what we were to do so that the FBI would share the urgency impressed on me. We left the meeting with the understanding that the FBI would take steps to make a polygraph machine and operator available early the following week if we needed it. Fred Buzhardt was to continue leading the investigation at the DOD, which had already shown some promise. At the end of the meeting

I reiterated the president's parting language to me about our responsibility to ferret out the leaker and to stop further leaks: "Goddamn it, we're not going to allow that. We're just not going to allow it."

5

A PROPOSAL GONE AWRY

After the meeting in the Roosevelt Room, I confirmed with Haig that he would monitor Buzhardt's investigation at the DOD. Young agreed to track the follow-up work with Haig. If the DOD investigation was successful in identifying the individual who leaked the SALT I fallback position, the dragnet type of polygraphing that the president was so adamant in pushing could be avoided. With that investigative course under way, I set about with Young to prepare the SIU team for further work.

We were given direct orders from the president to get to the bottom of both the Ellsberg case and the SALT I leak, and this work would require us to be able to read highly classified and sensitive information. Our unit was also tasked with finding out whether the Kennedy

administration was somehow involved in the assassina-
tion of President Diem in South Vietnam in 1963, part
of the president's ongoing preoccupation with uncovering wrongdoing and incompetence in earlier administra-
tions. Another area of interest for the president was the
Kennedy administration's disastrous handling of the Bay
of Pigs invasion in Cuba. To carry out all of these highly
sensitive investigations, we concluded that we would
need clearances from the initiating agencies to read some
of the most sensitive, highly classified memoranda and
back-channel cable traffic.

At this time in the Plumbers' operation, I wasn't able to
differentiate between matters of national security considerations and matters that were primarily political. My inability to clearly delineate these considerations may have
stemmed from the president's own views, in which his political survival and well-being were conflated with his idea
of a national security imperative. We certainly didn't take
the time to analyze what could appropriately be done by
the president as commander in chief under the Constitution, what he could do as head of the executive branch,
and what he could do as the political leader of his party
and future candidate for a second term of office. We simply charged forward without thinking about these critical
distinctions. To do our work, we needed higher security
clearances.

As a requirement for our respective jobs in Treasury
(Liddy), the CIA (Hunt), and the White House (Young

and myself), we had already received clearances to read classified information up to and including top secret information. As Kissinger's personal aide, Young had already received clearances higher than top secret, including some of the most sensitive classified clearances in the U.S. government. Liddy and I needed these additional clearances to handle the material for our work. Before we could get them, the CIA sent a man to brief us on these higher levels of security information. After showing us his identification, he explained the highly sensitive nature of the classified information, which could be accessed only with appropriate code words. After showing us some of the highly sensitive information we then had access to, including incredibly clear satellite-acquired photography of people and vehicles, the CIA briefer solemnly administered confidentiality oaths to us. We signed papers promising never to disclose this type of information in the future.

With the CIA security briefing behind us, we were now cleared to handle the classified information of most concern to the unit. First, however, we needed to "harden" the security of room 16 to ensure that other White House staff members, wandering visitors, or occasional media representatives did not gain access to it. We needed a safe place to meet and maintain our files. To this end, we sent a request through Haldeman's office to the technical services division of the Secret Service to install a motion-detection system in room 16 that would detect any unauthorized intruder. The system was up and running within two days of our request. Unfortunately, the system was so sensitive that if a paper floated off the top of a file because of a change in pressure in the ventilation system, an alarm would ring in the Secret Service command post in the EOB and an armed agent would run down to check on the office. Several false alarms brought agents to check up on these errant flying documents. We were encouraged to make sure everything in room 16 was stowed safely away at the end of each day and before we armed the system for its night's work.

On July 29, 1971, the president sent a letter to FBI director Hoover, at the request of Young and me, advising him that I had been directed to examine in depth the circumstances of the many disclosures of top secret and other sensitive information to the public. Young, Liddy, and I felt that unless the president weighed in with Hoover, we were unlikely to get the kind of aggressive investigation the president wanted. In a letter dated August 3, 1971, Hoover acknowledged the president's letter. He attached the results of five completed interviews with individuals named on a list of seventeen persons identified in an attachment to the president's letter. He also included a background paper on Daniel Ellsberg that we had requested. Hoover asked for my concurrence to conduct the remaining interviews, except for Dr. Ellsberg, which I granted. All of the enclosures were classified. This August 3 letter from Hoover didn't exhibit the urgency we felt was necessary.

In a meeting of the SIU during the week of July 26,

Liddy, Young, and I had asked ourselves whether the Bureau was proceeding on a "Bureau special" basis as they were supposed to be doing. A Bureau special involves a major commitment of resources in the FBI, and we weren't sure the Ellsberg/Pentagon Papers investigation was receiving that commitment. Lots of paper flowed to us from the Bureau, but that didn't mean an aggressive investigation was really underway. Liddy took on the task of finding out. In his career with the FBI, Liddy knew the difference between a normal FBI investigation and one that had the full support of Hoover and his principal deputies. He told us what it was like to be on a Bureau special investigation, and based on what we were seeing from the Bureau, this didn't seem to be one.

In meetings Liddy set up with his Bureau contacts during the weeks of July 26 and August 2, he learned that the Bureau was definitely not proceeding on any kind of special basis. Liddy's report to us about this deficiency was an important factor in the self-help mentality that then began to emerge in the unit. Rather than questioning the Bureau's lack of support, we resolved to go forward on our own with the investigation.

Liddy's memorandum of August 2, 1971, detailed his conversation with William Sullivan, the assistant director of the FBI, who led Liddy to believe that there was a general breakdown of capacity within the Bureau. Although I wondered whether Sullivan might have been trying to curry favor with the White House, hoping to succeed

Hoover, I considered him to be a credible and reliable person. This memo was forwarded to Ehrlichman and then to the president. A copy found its way to the attorney general and then to Robert Mardian. Overall, the memorandum was a scathing indictment of Bureau practices and the failure of leadership under Hoover.

Liddy's memo was prepared right at the time when Congressman Hale Boggs (D-La.) leveled an attack against Hoover and the Bureau and called for a congressional investigation. According to another report from Liddy, Deputy Attorney General Richard Kleindienst's initial support for a congressional investigation of the FBI was shut down when Hoover called the president to let him know that, if called to testify, Hoover would be forced to testify about "all" he knew about the Bureau's national security investigations. I understood this to mean that Hoover would disclose the warrantless wiretaps that the Bureau had implemented at White House insistence before the SIU was created. The congressional investigation did not go forward. Liddy's report further undermined my confidence that the Bureau could be trusted to carry forward the Pentagon Papers investigation effectively. If Hoover was willing to blackmail the president to avoid embarrassment, we asked ourselves, what else might he be prepared to do if he got crosswise with the White House?

The SIU members felt we needed an assessment of

Ellsberg's mental state to help us determine the likelihood that he would release other classified information. We had determined that as an employee at the RAND Corporation, a think tank and major defense contractor, Ellsberg probably had access to a wide assortment of classified documents. We were concerned that he might have had access to Nixon's current Vietnam War plans (from 1969 to 1971) that contained some of the most sensitive information in the government. We also felt that a psychological profile would provide fuel to discredit Ellsberg.

Obtaining information that could be used to discredit Ellsberg was the specific assignment of Hunt, who was reporting directly to Colson. Colson was the White House staff lead on getting derogatory information on any topic into the public arena, either through congressional hearings or through friendly reporters. The grist of the information that the unit felt could discredit Ellsberg was any connection with the Soviet Union.

Ellsberg had been seeing a psychiatrist by the name of Dr. Lewis Fielding for a number of years. Without knowing that psychiatrists rarely keep written notes about their patients (an "oh no, you're kidding me" type of fact that I learned from Jerry Jaffe, my White House colleague and best psychiatrist friend, long after the Pentagon Papers case was resolved), the unit assumed that the files maintained by Fielding would yield a treasure trove of information about Ellsberg. They might even include indications from Ellsberg that he was allied in some way with individuals who were giving information to the KGB and were working on behalf of the Soviet Union. When we asked the FBI for the results of its interview with Fielding in early August, we were told that no information was available. Fielding had quite properly refused on the grounds of doctor-patient privilege to reveal any information about Ellsberg to the Bureau.

The CIA psychological profile of Ellsberg that we had requested from the CIA turned out to be shallow and unsatisfactory. Even though Young had explained to the agency the importance we placed on getting in-depth information, nothing came back that was of any use. We had struck out working through both the FBI and the CIA. The self-help attitude that we were all feeling now ripened into a serious proposal.

In a meeting among all members of the unit, we discussed the specific steps we felt we could take to get the background we needed on Ellsberg. It was then, during the first week of August, that the idea of a covert operation first surfaced. The idea originated with either Liddy or Hunt.

In one of our planning sessions in room 16, Liddy explained to Young and me that he had been directly involved in several so-called black bag jobs as an FBI agent. He knew firsthand about several covert operations that had involved entering foreign embassies and consulates for the purpose of acquiring national security information. In these operations, the FBI would quietly inform the local police about an area surrounding the target embassy or consulate so they would stay away while the FBI black bag job was being conducted. He told us these operations were carried out when the national security interests were very strong. Given the president's clear directive that we were working on a matter of the highest national security importance, and with his charge to us to move forward with all resources available, we felt that a covert operation would be necessary and defensible. During deliberations, no one in the SIU questioned the necessity, legitimacy, legality, or morality of our proposed solution.

It was in this context that on August 11, Young drafted and I cosigned a memorandum to Ehrlichman. We recommended in paragraph two of our memo that "a covert operation be undertaken to examine all the medical files still held by Ellsberg's psychoanalyst covering the two-year period in which he was undergoing analysis." In the line below the recommendation, we set out two potential responses: APPROVE_____ DISAPPROVE_____. Ehrlichman wrote his initial "E" after APPROVE and then wrote in longhand beneath his approval: "if done under your assurance that it is not traceable."

The fifth paragraph, a section that was redacted in most copies of this memorandum because of national security concerns, recommended that contacts be made with MI-5, the British government's counterespionage agency, to determine whether the agency had "overheard" (wiretapped) Ellsberg at any time during his student days at Cambridge. Hunt felt that it was plausible that Ellsberg might have been "turned" by Soviet intelligence while a Cambridge student. He explained that a few brilliant British students, Kim Philby in particular, had been brought into the Soviet fold while studying at Cambridge. They had risen to high positions in government and British society, where they became notorious spies for the Soviet Union. In Hunt's view, it was clearly in the interest of the Soviets to undermine the U.S. war effort in Vietnam.

Ellsberg was obviously a brilliant man and had been a star student at Harvard and Cambridge. If the Soviets had turned him there, it would help explain how he had arranged a transfer of a full set of the Pentagon Papers to the Soviet embassy before they were published by *The New York Times*. According to Hunt, proof that he had colluded with the Soviets would have gone far to discredit Ellsberg personally and undermine his standing as a moral antiwar activist. My reading of the Hiss case in *Six Crises* inspired this speculative track of thinking among our unit's members and helps explain why this recommendation was included in the August 11 memorandum.

With Ehrlichman's approval of the covert operation recommended in paragraph two of the August 11 memorandum, the wheels were set in motion to carry it out. We did not analyze any of the potential consequences of this operation, and we did not comprehend that we were sowing poisonous seeds that would deform the Nixon ad-ministration, leading to its eventual demise.

As soon as I received Ehrlichman's approval in the memo, I called a meeting with Liddy, Hunt, and Young. We laid out the steps that we needed to take to put together a suc-cessful covert operation to examine Fielding's psychiatric files about Ellsberg.

We agreed that it would be necessary to undertake a reconnaissance mission to evaluate the obstacles that would be faced getting into Fielding's office in a complex in Beverly Hills. Because Ehrlichman had specifically di-rected that the operation not be traceable, I felt it would require operatives who had no direct contact with White House staff.

Hunt informed us that in his capacity as an agent with the CIA he had worked closely with a team of Cuban Americans—Bernard Barker, Felipe de Diego, and Eu-genio Martinez—who had varying degrees of background and experience in CIA operations and methods. (Their co-conspirator in the Watergate break-ins, Frank Sturgis, was yet to join the Plumbers team.) Hunt had worked to over-turn Castro with "the Cubans," as they became known in Watergate reporting, including in the failed Bay of Pigs operation that saw CIA employees training Cuban exiles in an Eisenhower-era plot to invade Cuba. He felt that his former colleagues would be willing to help us carry out this operation; Martinez alone had completed hundreds of missions infiltrating Cuba. But first, we needed to scope out the area and understand the requirements.

Hunt recommended that we request support from the CIA in performing the reconnaissance. We asked Ehrlichman to contact General Robert Cushman, the deputy director of the CIA, to obtain technical support for the mission and for any follow-up work that might need to be done. That we were openly requesting assistance from the CIA indicated our belief that we were engaged in a legitimate national security investigation and that we weren't playing outside the rules. Even though we knew the CIA didn't have jurisdiction on U.S. soil, we felt we could still use their equipment without compromising the Agency. Hunt persuaded us that since he and his team would not be working for the CIA, mere use of CIA equipment would not violate the prohibition on Agency activity within the United States.

When he called Cushman, Ehrlichman told him that Hunt had been hired by the White House staff in a security capacity. Ehrlichman asked for Cushman's support for work that Hunt might do as part of the White House staff. The CIA arranged for one of its technical specialists to meet Hunt and Liddy in a D.C. safe house. Both were given an alias and documentation, and Liddy was given a small camera to use in photographing the office area. Hunt and Liddy were also given disguise materials, including an ill-fitting red wig for Hunt and Coke-bottle-thick glasses for Liddy. Liddy also received a gait-altering device.

On August 25, Liddy and Hunt left for California and checked into the Beverly Hilton hotel. Hunt told me he wanted to have an individual in California available to the team in case an emergency arose, so he contacted Morton "Tony" Jackson, a Beverly Hills attorney who had worked with Hunt in the CIA. They explained to Jackson that they were conducting a sensitive drug control operation.

The day after meeting with Jackson, Liddy and Hunt went to Fielding's office and surveyed it from many directions, using what they claimed was "good tradecraft." They took photographs of Fielding's building and posed Liddy in the foreground, like a tourist, with the office in the background.

In an example of somewhat less-skilled tradecraft, they left the film of Liddy posing in front of Fielding's office in the camera. The camera was returned to the CIA with the incriminating film still inside. While this appeared to be a major breach in operational security, we were assuming at the time that the CIA was on the same team as the White House staff and would not be looking for ways to undermine a project that had such strong presidential support.

I learned later that inside the CIA there was some grave concern that supporting the SIU could be seen as a CIA violation of the statutory limitations on domestic activities. There was legitimate fear of vulnerability for the

Agency if it was associated in some way with clandestine domestic operations.

That same evening, Hunt and Liddy conducted a more thorough reconnaissance of the building. They wanted to understand the clinic crew's and the janitors' schedules. Hunt also talked to a Latina cleaning woman in Spanish, who opened Dr. Fielding's door for them so that they could photograph the interior. Apparently she believed their story that they were doctors who needed to leave an urgent message for Fielding. Hunt tipped her for her help. Soon thereafter they left for the airport and returned to D.C.

The CIA technical-support person met them at Dulles to pick up the camera and film, which the CIA subsequently developed. Very few of the pictures turned out because of a camera malfunction and low light conditions. However, the photo of Liddy posing in Fielding's parking space came out bright and clear.

Liddy and Hunt formulated an operational plan and gave it to Young and me the day after their return. Young and I felt we needed to communicate with Ehrlichman further before we gave the final green light for the break-in. We told Liddy and Hunt that they were not to go into the Fielding office building themselves. Only Hunt's team should be directly involved in carrying out the operation.

Hunt then contacted his team of Barker, Diego, and Martinez. When I asked Hunt how much it would cost to hire the team, he told me they would not take compensation beyond their immediate expenses. He had explained to them that this operation served the national security of the country. The three of them felt that it was their patriotic duty to support the mission. Hunt also told me that Martinez was a particularly skilled covert operator who had surreptitiously entered Cuba over thirty-five times during the previous ten years. Hunt was pleased that Martinez was on the team to support Barker and Diego. All three would later be prosecuted for their involvement in the Fielding operation.

I asked Hunt and Liddy for the total cost of the operation—plane fare, hotel, equipment. They thought $2,000 in cash would cover it. I called Colson and told him we were ready to go forward with an effort to acquire some information about Ellsberg, and that I would need some operational money to carry it out. Colson told me he would get those funds for me, and that they would be delivered by an intermediary some time the next day.

Two days before the operation, on Wednesday, September 1, there was a knock on the door of a little-used, poorly marked back entrance to my office. I had told Colson that whoever was to deliver the funds was to use that back entrance and not go through the regular entrance where my secretary worked. I also did not want the funds delivered to room 16, which we had kept as secret as we could from other members of the White House staff and other visitors.

I got up from my desk and opened the door a crack. A

man I didn't know quietly handed me an envelope, turned around quickly, and left.

The next day Young came to my office for our final communication with Ehrlichman, who was vacationing on Cape Cod with his wife. We put a call through to him and told him we were ready to "go forward" in California. I kept the conversation general and avoided saying anything specific, owing to the public nature of the phone call. I also assumed that he was familiar enough with the practices of a covert operation that he would understand what we were asking him to approve. I didn't feel it was necessary to describe the details of the operation in this final communication, in part because we already had his written approval and active involvement in calling the CIA for logistical support. At Young's request, Ehrlichman had also asked Colson for an outline of how he intended to use the information obtained from Hunt and Liddy's operation. During the phone call, Ehrlichman confirmed to Young and me that we should go forward and let him know what information we acquired.

Hunt and Liddy were waiting impatiently in room 16 for the money and this final approval. They were impatient because it was getting close to time to leave and they needed preparation time to conduct the operation that Labor Day weekend. After getting off the phone with Ehrlichman, I took the money to Liddy and told him to make sure that he exchanged the bills for others to prevent any kind of tracing. My instructions to them were to call me at my home in Crystal City as soon as the operation was over. I told Liddy and Hunt, "For God's sake, don't get caught."

OVER THE NEXT two days, Liddy and Hunt flew first to Chicago, where they acquired walkie-talkies for the entry operation, and then to Los Angeles, using their aliases provided by the CIA. The operation went forward on the evening of Friday, September 3, right before Labor Day weekend. Following the plan they had presented to us, they went to Fielding's office and discovered that the door to the building was locked, despite preparations to make sure it was unlocked. To gain entry, they broke an external window that was shielded by trees, hoping to make it look as if there had been a burglary to steal drugs from a doctor's office. During the search of Fielding's office, Barker, Diego, and Martinez spread papers and pills around, doing further damage to the office. They took Polaroid pictures of the damage they inflicted.

Their operation turned up no information or files relevant to Daniel Ellsberg.

Meanwhile, I was in my fiber-backed rocking chair in my apartment in Crystal City, Virginia, rocking back and forth and waiting for the call from Liddy. It was well past 1:00 A.M. EST when Liddy finally called to report that they had gotten in and out cleanly, but that no mother lode of information about Ellsberg was found. He promised a full report on his return.

While waiting for Liddy's call, I had imagined getting a chilling report from the Beverly Hills Police Department informing me that they had five men under arrest who had given the police my name and telephone number. So I was as relieved as I had ever been in my life to know that they had made it out of the building without getting caught. However, I sensed then—but did not fully comprehend—that something irrevocable had occurred.

ON SUNDAY, SEPTEMBER 5, Hunt and Liddy returned to D.C., but I didn't see Liddy until Tuesday. I met him in room 16, where he showed me the Polaroid photographs of the damage inflicted on the office. I was stunned and appalled. I couldn't understand what was unclear about the word "covert" in "covert operation." Liddy said that making the operation look like a drug burglary gone awry would make it less traceable to the White House. Liddy showed me the tools and the lethal-looking combat knife that he had carried during the operation. I asked him if he would have used the knife if he or the team seemed threatened; he assured me he would have killed if necessary. This admission shocked me: I had simply not envisioned any potential violence, particularly violence that could have led to someone's death.

It is true that I wasn't an expert in covert operations, and that seeing the evidence of the damage affected me much more than the theory and planning had. That Liddy would have killed somebody if necessary seemed to be far in excess of what Young or I had contemplated. The recognition that the operation could have resulted in such a dire outcome made me deeply question whether we were on the right course. As Liddy pointed out to me later, I was not prepared for the real possibility that a covert operation could result in fatalities. Feeling disappointed by the failure of their mission, Liddy suggested that he and Hunt go back to California to look for Ellsberg's files in Dr. Fielding's home. I was noncommittal and said I needed to talk to Ehrlichman before giving an answer.

On September 8, I took the photographs to Ehrlichman to report what had happened. He too seemed shocked and surprised by the extent of the damage in the operation and told me to shut down any further investigation of Ellsberg through covert operations. He added that what he was seeing was beyond the scope of what he had approved. I told him it was beyond the scope of what I had envisioned, too, and I agreed that we ought not authorize any further covert activity. I returned to room 16 later that day and informed Liddy and Hunt that Ehrlichman had rejected their suggestion about conducting a break-in of Dr. Fielding's apartment. With this decision, my involvement with the covert activities of the Plumbers came to an end.

The next day, Ehrlichman met with the president and reported to him that we had a "little operation in California" that had netted nothing, and that it was better that he not know about it. Then, on September 10, they met again and Ehrlichman recommended a covert operation into the National Archives. As recounted in *Abuse of Power: The New Nixon Tapes,* Ehrlichman said to the president, "There's a lot of hanky-panky with secret documents, and on the eve of the publication of the Pentagon Papers those three guys made a deposit into the National Archives, under an agreement, of a whole lot of papers. Now I'm going to steal those documents out of the National Archives." After an exchange of ideas about how to do it, Ehrlichman continued, "Yeah. And nobody can tell we've been in there."

In 2007, I learned from John Powers, an archivist working with the Nixon Papers at the National Archives, that an operation at the National Archives was in fact carried out. Whoever was responsible for this operation did not work with me in the Plumbers group.

Over the next two months, the SIU focused on other leaks besides the Pentagon Papers. However, my time was completely taken up with the implementation of the Cabinet Committee for International Narcotics Control.

The Fielding break-in on September 3, 1971, concluded the seven-week period that doomed Nixon's presidency, though it would not be clear for three more years. Nixon was first reelected by a landslide. But the moral authority of his administration had been terminally compromised. In those seven weeks, the SIU had undergone a journey from suspicion to certainty to covert action to frustration to zealotry: hardened by their first action, the Plumbers knew that the rules of engagement had changed and the conventional respect for laws set aside. A botched break-in, evidenced in a few Polaroids, didn't seem to represent much. In practice, however, it was the first step on the path that led a presidency to run out of control.

6

BLIND LOYALTY ENSNARES ME IN WATERGATE

During the last week of October 1971, John Dean, the president's counsel, informed me that Jeb Magruder was looking for legal help with some sort of intelligence program. Magruder was a political operative who had served the president in a variety of capacities and was now deputy director of the Committee for the Re-election of the President (CRP, but better known as CREEP among those less likely to be fans). I was unhappy with the clandestine activities we had carried out and also felt that this was more naturally an opportunity for Liddy, since working in the presidential campaign would use skills that he had already developed as a candidate while running for office in New York's Twenty-eighth Congressional district. I asked him to come meet with me and Dean, who would explain to him what Magruder had in mind.

After explaining the scope of the potential political-intelligence operation and the substantial money it would need, Dean indicated that Liddy would need to leave the White House to carry it out. I agreed. Liddy told me he had come to the White House because of Attorney General Mitchell, that he worked for Ehrlichman and me, and he wanted assurance that his going to CRP had everyone's approval. I checked with Ehrlichman, who in turn got Mitchell's concurrence to offer Liddy the position of general counsel to the 1972 campaign. Liddy was now on his way out of the SIU and the White House. After arrangements for his move to CRP were made, I called Magruder and told him Liddy would require close supervision. I did not go into any detail, which I regret, but I did indicate that close monitoring of Liddy's activities would be important.

In early December 1971, a leak appeared in Jack Anderson's column in *The Washington Post* regarding the India-Pakistan conflict. There was information suggesting that the source of the leak was within the National Security Council staff.

At the beginning of the investigation, Young felt that it was necessary to put a warrantless national security wiretap on the home telephone of a yeoman who worked on the NSC staff. We had learned that this yeoman had reproduced documents from Kissinger's briefcase and made them available to an admiral assigned to the NSC staff by the chairman of the Joint Chiefs of Staff. This raised the specter that there was a Pentagon spy ring setting up double agents to steal secrets from the NSC.

In my view, the warrantless wiretap did not appear to be necessary. I received a call from Ehrlichman while I was attending a meeting at one of the office buildings on Lafayette Square. He asked me whether I agreed with Young's recommendation to institute the wiretap. I said I did not, and he told me that as of that time I was relieved of any further participation in the SIU and that Young would carry on this task by himself.

I learned later that Young completed an extremely thorough and comprehensive investigation, amassing a foot-thick stack of documents, including the results of the wiretaps, interrogations, and cables related to this operation. This massive report on the investigation has never been made available to the public.

The Watergate story has been thoroughly described in many books, with excellent coverage in *All the President's Men* by Bob Woodward and Carl Bernstein. Many principals—Ehrlichman, Magruder, Liddy, even Nixon—wrote biographies with their opinions about Watergate and what happened. From the perspective of those in the White House, it was a difficult, chaotic time.

On June 19, 1972, a story appeared in the *St. Louis Post-Dispatch*. I remember walking through the Chase Park Plaza hotel in St. Louis, where I was staying for a while attending a seminar. The front-page story caught my eye. It detailed who was caught in a break-in at the Watergate Hotel in D.C. While I had no knowledge of the planning for or execution of the Watergate break-in, I speculated that by sheer force of his will, Liddy had persuaded Magruder to approve a break-in at the Watergate Complex.

At the conclusion of the seminar, I asked my wife Suzanne to join me in St. Louis so we could drive back to D.C. together. On the way back, we stopped over in southern Indiana. Because I had been out of touch for two weeks, I put a call through to the White House for an update on what was happening. My secretary told me John Dean was trying urgently to get in touch with me.

I called Dean, and what he said caused me to recoil. He said we had some major problems brewing based on some "activities" that had happened. He was very cryptic, but I understood exactly what he meant. I went back to the car and told Suzanne about Dean's fears. At that time, I hadn't told her the full extent of my involvement; much of what we did was kept secret even from our own families.

After returning to D.C., I met with Dean right away. He gave me some background on what had happened in the Watergate event and told me he had become aware of some of the activities of the SIU in 1971. I told him that in 1971, it was my belief that everything we did was of the highest national security importance, and that I still believed that to be true. Dean said the White House strategy was to suppress any information that would link

Watergate with the White House or anything that had occurred the previous year.

I told Dean that I felt bound by the secrecy requirement imposed on the unit, and that everything I had done had been carried out under intense pressure to achieve results and high national security stakes emphasized by the president. This pressure had come directly from the Oval Office. He nodded as I said this.

Then he told me we were going to have a rough ride.

During the course of the Watergate investigation, the U.S. attorney Earl Silbert decided to question some White House staffers on their knowledge about Watergate. Dean arranged for some staff members to be interviewed rather than be required to go before a grand jury. He arranged for me to be interviewed at the Department of Justice by an assistant U.S. attorney. Dean told me he had secured the agreement of the U.S attorney that no national-security-related questions would be asked, and that if any national security questions were asked, I would have to avoid answering them. He made it clear that disclosure of any of the SIU activities in 1971 would be dangerous and unacceptable. Dean specifically advised me that the Fielding incident was not relevant to Watergate and would not be touched upon in the deposition.

The assistant U.S. attorney who conducted the deposition told me he was not interested in pursuing national security matters. I was, however, asked if I had any knowledge of travel by Hunt and Liddy to California in 1971. I answered the questions by interpreting them as referring to national security, so I said I wasn't aware of any travel to California. As I pointed out in my statement to the court in 1974, "This interpretation was highly strained, reflecting a desperate effort on my part to avoid any possible disclosure of the work of the unit in accordance with the instructions of the president that had been relayed to me by Mr. Ehrlichman." This was confirmed by Dean just before the deposition.

The reason for the question about the California travel? The U.S. attorney was in possession of the photograph that was left in the camera by Liddy and Hunt. The CIA had forwarded the photograph to the DOJ.

After the deposition, I had no further contact with the U.S. attorney or anyone else regarding the work of the SIU. From my perspective at the time, it was a finished operation. I felt that those who were involved in it—Young, Liddy, Hunt, Barker, Diego, and Martinez—were all subject to the same secrecy requirements that I was. I also felt, naively, that this secrecy requirement would carry through any of the investigations into Watergate that involved some of the former SIU members.

The task of implementing the strategy of suppressing knowledge of White House involvement in any of those activities fell to Dean. He received that thankless task even though (as far as I know) he had no involvement in any of the actual criminal acts of the SIU in 1971 or of the Watergate team from CRP in 1972.

Following the 1972 election, which Nixon won overwhelmingly against Senator George McGovern, I felt a great desire to leave the White House and to serve in one of the departments far removed from law enforcement, narcotics control, or clandestine activity. While I had told my friend Ray Hanzlik, a former schoolmate and colleague on the White House staff, that only a yo-yo would take a position in the Department of Transportation (DOT), I had become increasingly interested in transportation policy. As White House liaison to the District of Columbia, I worked to resuscitate the appropriations bill for the D.C. Metro, which had been stalemated in Congress.

When I told Ehrlichman about my interest in Transportation, he wasn't initially enthusiastic. He told me I would have to explain to the president why I wanted to go to DOT and arranged for me to take a helicopter ride to Camp David three weeks after the election, when Nixon was in deep retreat preparing for his second term. When I got to Camp David and went to the president's cabin, his personal valet Manuel "Manolo" Sanchez ushered me into the living room. The president was sitting a few feet away from a crackling fire. He smiled and waved me to the chair opposite him.

"So why do you want to go over to Transportation?"

I told him I felt Transportation was dealing with some of the more interesting domestic issues that I had been involved in. While it was a new department, I thought it had a great mission in funding urban mass transit and upgrading the federal aviation system, and that I had always had great respect for the Coast Guard. I told the president I had really enjoyed my work on the White House staff, but that I wanted to participate more directly with Congress and the many interest groups that were engaged in transportation policy.

He looked at me without much enthusiasm, then said, "Well, if that's what you want, it's OK with me." In a later memo, Haldeman wrote that the president felt there were more important things for "Bud to do," but that he (Haldeman) thought going to Transportation was a good idea for now.

When I left Camp David, I was assured that the president would send my nomination forward to the Senate very quickly. I was nominated for the position of undersecretary of transportation in December 1972.

Lynn Sutcliffe, one of my best friends from law school, was also working in D.C. at the time. He had been editor in chief while I was notes editor of the University of Washington Law Review and was now a senior staff member on the Senate Commerce Committee. As soon as Lynn received my nomination, he started preparing the questions that I would be asked in an open hearing before the Senate Commerce Committee.

The Watergate investigation was in full swing, and I was clearly concerned about the kinds of questions that I might get. While the work with the Plumbers was a small fraction of my time, increasing investigation pressures were impacting already fragile relationships within the White House. Fortunately, I'd had no contact with Liddy since he had left the White House in December 1971, so there was no record of discussion with him about Watergate that could have been used to justify questions by the senators on the committee.

The day that I testified before the committee was one of the more intense days of my life. A good friend of mine who had served on the D.C. City Council, Tedson Meyers, gave very supportive opening remarks about my nomination. Tedson was one of the finest men I had ever known. He and I had worked on many issues related to the District of Columbia, including law enforcement and his initiative to make the walkways of the District suitable for handicapped people. Some other introductory comments were offered by senators Warren Magnusson and Henry "Scoop" Jackson because I was a resident of Washington State.

Most of the questions from the senators focused on transportation issues that I would face as undersecretary. However, I did get some questions about the organization and activities of the SIU. I answered all of them accurately and truthfully and denied any knowledge of any bugging or electronic surveillance by the SIU. I had been removed from the unit before any of those activities took place. At the end of all the questioning, I received unanimous confirmation for my position as undersecretary of transportation in January 1973.

On February 4, 1973, Suzanne and I dined as guests of the president at an elegant seven-course candlelit dinner in the State Dining Room of the White House. Each table was attended by two formally dressed waiters and waitresses who served each course and filled our glasses. For most of the people in attendance, it was a festive evening of tinkling crystal, shared memories of the previous five years, and warm toasts—but not for me. Although I was there to celebrate my confirmation as undersecretary of the Department of Transportation as well as the confirmations of my fellow cabinet and subcabinet colleagues, my mood at dinner, far from ebullient, was dark and full of foreboding. The dinner was the culmination of my quest for high position and power that had begun five years earlier and had resulted in my appointment as undersecretary at the young age of thirty-three. Unlike most of the celebrants that evening, a few others and I were skating on ice slowly melting from the heat of the Watergate investigation.

In May 1973, the ice cracked open and I fell through. Then, after months of guilt and sleepless nights, a Thanksgiving trip to Williamsburg in late November 1973 finally made me face the errors in my thinking as the head of the SIU.

7

PLEADING GUILTY

In *Man's Search for Meaning,* Viktor Frankl asserts that in every situation, there is only one right answer. The challenge is how to work your way through to it. And that one right answer, no matter how difficult a choice, is the answer that will have the greatest integrity.

In the late afternoon of November 23, 1973, I stood on the lawn of the House of Burgesses, the former legislature in Colonial Williamsburg, Virginia. At the invitation of the president of the College of William and Mary and his wife, I had brought my family to Williamsburg as a respite from the Watergate storms that had deluged the capital.

This was a difficult time, when my despair over the course of my legal defense was causing me sharp pangs of conscience. On May 2, 1973, not even four months into the job, I had resigned from my position as undersecretary of transportation, a casualty of the exploding Watergate investigation.

When I approved the covert operation in Dr. Lewis Fielding's office in 1971, national security was my main concern; I was able to convince myself that it was the right thing to do under the circumstances. Later, I relied on national security to justify lying to an assistant U.S. attorney during the Watergate investigation about my knowledge of the Plumbers' activities.

As I prepared my defense, again, national security was my justification. But as I worked through the issues, I felt uncomfortable with the soundness of this defense. The more I tried to align my thought with a higher sense of right, the more problematic it became.

Looking around me, I recognized that my family and I were benefiting from rights that emanated from the founding ideals of America. Despite being under indictment in both federal and state courts, and publicly identified with serious crimes, I enjoyed the freedom to travel wherever I wanted, to speak with whomever I wished, to pray freely in any church, and to talk to the press. Benefiting from all these things, I had nonetheless violated another man's civil rights. This seemed hypocritical regardless of my belief that it was in the best interests of national defense.

I came to accept that I could no longer defend my conduct. If I defended myself further, if I continued to justify violating rights I continued to enjoy, I would not only be a hypocrite but a traitor to the fundamental American idea of the right of an individual to be free from unwarranted government intrusion. It was then and there, in Colonial Williamsburg, surrounded by family and a sense of the history of America, that I decided to plead guilty.

My wife Suzanne and I had discussed the implications of pleading guilty, what it would mean for our boys and our family. The choice was not one between how the boys might be hurt by having a father who did or didn't go to prison. Rather, the choice was between a father who ran away from responsibility or a father who did the best he could to uphold the freedoms this country stands for. In any other country, I would already have been arrested—and we both recognized the importance of protecting American freedoms for everyone, Ellsberg and Fielding especially. My only choice was to try to serve time honorably.

Three days later, my attorney, Steve Shulman, and I walked into the reception room of the office of Leon Jaworski, the special prosecutor for Watergate and related crimes. While I was convinced of the rightness of the decision I'd made in Williamsburg, I felt nervous and fearful about how the meeting would go.

Jaworski had been appointed the special prosecutor six weeks before our meeting, after President Nixon had accepted the resignations of Attorney General Elliot Richardson and Deputy Attorney General William Ruckelshaus for their refusal to fire Archibald Cox, the previous special prosecutor, who had ultimately resigned as well. (These dismissals became known as the "Saturday Night Massacre.") Jaworski had a reputation for toughness and fairness, partly from his work on the U.S. prosecution staff at the war crimes trials in Nuremberg, Germany. During my meeting with him that day, and on other occasions several years later, I also learned that he was a compassionate man who deeply loved his country and hated those who abused its trust.

After waiting a few minutes, instead of the standard hour that prosecutors often make suspects wait, Jaworski welcomed me into his stark temporary office. Jaworski was joined by William Merrill, the lawyer directly assigned to prosecute the White House Plumbers.

Steve explained to the prosecutors that we had reviewed and analyzed my case from every possible perspective. He told them we had reached a decision to initiate steps with the special prosecutor that would settle the various charges without requiring a criminal trial.

After a few quiet moments, Jaworski asked, "Is this your view, Mr. Krogh?"

"Yes, sir, it is."

"Would you please tell me how you came to this decision?"

I told Jaworski that ever since the president had set up the Special Investigations Unit in 1971, and Ehrlichman assigned me to it, I had justified what we did on the basis of national security, that the president himself had described the work of our unit as being crucial. That's why I thought that getting all the information we could about Dr. Ellsberg and why he released the Pentagon Papers was serving a national security purpose. And since covert operations had been done in the past for national security, I felt that a covert entry into Dr. Fielding's office to get information about Dr. Ellsberg was justifiable. I added that the more I had thought about it, the clearer I had seen that even though there may well have been some damaging impacts to national security from Ellsberg's releasing the Pentagon Papers, those impacts simply could not justify the invasion of Fielding's rights that this operation involved. I said I didn't feel I could defend my conduct any further because it violated a fundamental principle in our country: the right of an individual to be protected from an unlawful action by the government.

Jaworski and Merrill listened intently. It was clear they had discussed the procedure involved in my pleading guilty to the underlying constitutional crimes—deprivation of Dr. Fielding's civil rights to be free from an unlawful search.

"I think we need to get a little more specific, Mr. Krogh. Do I understand that you are prepared to plead guilty to deprivation of Fielding's rights? Is that so?" asked Jaworski.

Steve, aware that this was moving more quickly than he was comfortable with as my lawyer, jumped into the conversation. He told Jaworski that I felt I could no longer defend in conscience the Fielding break-in on the basis of national security. He hoped that if we could come to an agreement on my pleading guilty to the deprivation of civil rights charges that the false declaration indictment would be dismissed. He hoped that if I pled guilty to the civil rights charge, which carried a potential ten-year prison sentence, more than any of the lesser charges, that the lesser federal and state charges would be dropped.

For the first time in a long time, the rightness of my decision felt unambiguous. With a guilty plea, however, would come the sentencing process, and I wanted to avoid the appearance that I had sold out my colleagues and friends to receive a reduced sentence. I believed that the truth was of paramount importance, but that it would be wrong for me to directly benefit from sharing a truth that would damage others. I was concerned about how Jaworski and Merrill would respond to my thoughts on the matter, but unless I had their agreement, I couldn't go forward.

I made very clear that my plea of guilty was conditional on the prosecutors agreeing that I not talk with them or the grand jury until after I'd been sentenced. It was critically important to me that U.S. district judge Gerhard Gesell sentence me solely on the basis of what I did, not what I might say that would implicate others. Even though I understood that others were eager to testify and give up evidence in exchange for a lighter sentence, I couldn't stand the idea. I gave him my word that once sentenced, I would tell them the truth.

Jaworski and Merrill assured me that they would think about my offer to plead guilty before testifying and get back to me quickly. After some hesitation, Jaworski asked me if I had heard of Albert Speer and how he dealt with the prosecution at Nuremberg. He went on to explain that while the gravity of Albert Speer's actions in Hitler's Third Reich was vastly different, there was a similar principle at stake: we are all responsible for our own actions, and we can't justify criminal conduct on the basis that we were ordered to do so or felt compelled by circumstances. Jaworski said those who prosecuted Speer (including Jaworski) had felt he had made an honest effort to take some responsibility for his actions. It sounded to Jaworski as though my offer to plead guilty was an effort to do the same thing. I remembered that Speer was sentenced to twenty years in Spandau prison for his war crimes, and I hoped I would get less than the ten-year possible sentence for the crime I had committed.

One of the most important points I made to Jaworski was that while I felt I was not *exclusively* responsible for what the Plumbers did, I was nevertheless *fully* responsible. While the idea for the Fielding break-in originated with Hunt and Liddy, I fully endorsed their recommendation. In fact, I had pushed them hard for aggressive action without fully understanding what that might entail. Because I could have stopped the operation and didn't, I was fully responsible.

We left, and the next morning Steve called and asked

me to come and see him right away. During our darkest days together during the previous six months, Steve had always maintained a light spirit. At considerable financial sacrifice to himself, he had taken my case at the request of my friend Tedson Meyers. Despite the seriousness of our talks, Steve occasionally lightened things up with one-arm pushup competitions. As I crumpled to the floor, Steve would continue counting into the twenties, then switch arms.

Steve told me that Jaworski had accepted my offer to plead guilty, and that November 30 was the day we would go before Judge Gesell to enter the offer of the guilty plea. Steve added that Jaworski was willing to drop the false declaration charge, since the violation of Dr. Fielding's constitutional rights under the Fourth Amendment was much more serious and important than the false declaration charge.

In preparation for the plea in front of Judge Gesell, Steve and I wrote a statement for me to read in court. A few days later, Steve and I walked through a swarm of reporters, photographers, and cameramen and into the E. Barrett Prettyman Federal Courthouse in Washington, D.C. The courtroom was packed with reporters and other regulars who followed all Watergate press conferences, hearings, and court dramas like groupies trailing a rock band. Standing in front of Judge Gesell with Steve Shulman at my side, I read the following statement:

The sole basis for my defense was to have been that I acted in the interest of national security. However, upon serious and lengthy reflection, I now feel that the sincerity of my motivation cannot justify what was done and that I cannot in conscience assert national security as a defense. I am therefore pleading guilty because I have no defense to this charge. I will make a detailed statement as to my reasons which I will submit to the Court and make public prior to sentencing.

My decision is based upon what I think and feel is right and what I consider to be the best interests of the nation. The values expressed by Your Honor in the hearing on defense motions on November 13 particularly brought home to me the transcendent importance of the rule of law over the motivations of man.

I have expressed to the Special Prosecutor's office my desire that I not be required to testify in this area until after sentencing. My plea today is based on conscience, and I want to avoid any possible suggestion that I am seeking leniency through testifying. The Special Prosecutor's office has expressed no objection to this position.

My coming to this position today stems from my asking myself what ideas I wanted to stand for, what I wanted to represent to myself and to my family and to be identified with for the rest of my experience. I simply feel that what was done in the Ellsberg operation was in violation of what I perceive to be the fundamental idea in the character of this country—the paramount importance of the rights of the individual. I don't want to be associated with that violation any longer by attempting to defend it.

I had finally reached an understanding of the hole in my decision-making process, that what I had done wasn't right, and that it had a hugely negative impact on society. Despite the fear of what prison and life as a convicted felon might hold, my final decision to plead guilty was an important step in restoring some of my integrity.

A few weeks later, I sat down in a prayer meeting with former White House special counsel Colson, his Christian colleagues, and Senator Harold Hughes at Fellowship House in D.C. During our meeting, I explained to them why I felt it essential that I plead guilty and serve whatever sentence might be imposed. I was willing to accept any punishment that a court might impose. Moreover, as I had indicated to my friend David Eisenhower, I had pleaded guilty on the basis of conscience and did not want to be pardoned. Serving a prison sentence was an opportunity for me to pay part of the price that had to be paid for my misconduct.

Perhaps the most important step in my thought process was to get outside of the circumstances in which I had made my original decision. Specifically, I could see that my absolute loyalty to President Nixon, both personally and to his view of the national security threat, had skewed my perspective. This kind of loyalty lacked integrity because it was unbalanced and too exclusive. Loyalty to the president was obviously important up to a point. However, loyalty to the Constitution, to the rule of law, and to moral and ethical requirements should have been key factors in my decisions as well.

Groupthink also infected the decision-making of the Plumbers unit. Each of us brought to the work of the unit a high degree of zeal. We accepted the description of the threat without question, and we did not question each other on the rightness of the break-in or its necessity.

National security as I perceived it in 1971 was a monolithic concept. I accepted then that if the president invoked that term it meant that the threat to the nation's security was substantial and immediate. Upon pleading guilty, I realized that the term cannot be used as a blanket justification for any type of conduct to defend the nation's security.

SIX WEEKS LATER, before sentencing, I wrote to Judge Gesell in my "Statement of Defendant on the Offense and His Role" that "national security is obviously a fundamental goal and a proper concern of any country. It is also a concept that is subject to a wide range of definitions, a factor that makes all the more essential a painstaking approach to the definition of national security in any given instance." In responding to the national security threat, government officials must make painstaking efforts to ensure that they comply with the law.

Perhaps the simplest way to have reached the right decision at the time would have been to ask people who I knew had real integrity if this was the right decision. In the environment of secrecy within the White House, such advice would have been extremely difficult to seek.

On January 24, 1974, Suzanne and I drove in tense silence to Steve Shulman's office, where she could avoid the intense media scrum that awaited us at the courthouse. We had tried to prepare the boys for the worst—a possible ten-year sentence—something that my older son Peter could understand at age eight, Matthew much less so at age four. At my sentencing, I told Judge Gesell how deeply sorrowful I was over the suffering that many people had endured because of my offense. I noted that Dr. Fielding and Dr. Ellsberg, both of them, were deprived of rights to which they were entitled. I acknowledged that the American people felt confused and disturbed by what took place in the Fielding break-in, which raised many questions about what the country represented and what it meant. I said that no assertion of national security, no matter how deeply held, could change the fact that I had made a fundamental mistake.

Judge Gesell listened carefully and then responded:

Contrary to the public understanding, you were not involved in any other aspect of the various events being investigated by the Special Watergate Prosecutor. You received no money for your part in this affair. In acknowledging your guilt, you have made no effort, as you very well might have, to place the primary blame on others who initiated and who approved the undertaking. A wholly improper, illegal task was assigned to you by higher authority and you carried it out because of a combination of loyalty and I believe a degree of vanity, thereby compromising your obligations as a lawyer and as a public servant.

He then placed his decision in a broader legal context. He quoted Justice Louis Brandeis: "If the Government becomes a lawbreaker, it breeds contempt for the law. It invites every man to become a law unto himself. It invites anarchy."

The judge told me that because I was a lawyer and had held high responsibility when the offense occurred, any punishment short of jail would be inadequate. He then sentenced me to a term of two to six years, of which I was to serve six months and remain on unsupervised probation for another two years. Since I was the first person sentenced in the Watergate chaos, Judge Gesell could have set a stiffer sentence for me as an example for others who had also been indicted. I was grateful to be able to call home from the courthouse and let the boys know about the relatively short sentence.

PRECISELY EIGHT MONTHS later, on August 24, 1974, two weeks after his resignation, Richard Nixon and I met in San Clemente. During the course of a two-hour discussion, he asked me whether he had approved the break-in of Fielding's office. Perhaps he was unclear which break-ins he had knowledge of and had authorized. When I told him, no, he had not to my knowledge approved the covert operation into Fielding's office, he told me that had I asked him for his approval, I would have had it. But for me, by then, that was hardly the point.

8

FROM COURTHOUSE TO JAILHOUSE

"Are the cuffs too tight?" The United States marshal, a Black man with kind eyes, finished handcuffing me to a waist chain linked to shackles around each of my ankles. He had just led me from a solitary holding cell in the basement of the E. Barrett Prettyman Federal Courthouse in Washington, D.C., to a covered concourse where prisoners are driven in and out. At my sentencing hearing ten days before, U.S. district judge Gerhard Gesell had directed me to turn myself in to the U.S. marshals.

"No, not too tight," I answered. He gently took my arm and led me clanking to the standard-issue government sedan. He put his hand on my head as I ducked down and eased me into the back seat. The marshal and his partner, the driver, got in the front seats. The driver started the car immediately and pulled quickly out of the concourse, taking a left turn past a few lingering photographers and reporters milling around the entrance. He turned right onto Pennsylvania Avenue for a few blocks, skirted the Ellipse south of the White House and my former office, and headed northwest out the George Washington Parkway toward the Montgomery County jail in Rockville, Maryland.

As I was driven to Rockville, I reflected on the awful irony of going to jail for committing a serious federal crime when one of my principal responsibilities had been to reduce crime in the District of Columbia. Judge Gesell had sentenced me to two to six years in prison, suspending all of it except for six months, for violating the civil rights of Dr. Lewis Fielding, Dr. Daniel Ellsberg's psychiatrist.

For the brief four months I served as undersecretary of the Department of Transportation in 1973, I was provided "portal-to-portal" service. I was picked up at my home by a DOT driver, usually around 7:00 A.M., taken to the department headquarters building, and then driven home at the end of the day. Being driven from the Prettyman courthouse to the Rockville jail gave "portal-to-portal" a whole new meaning.

About forty minutes after leaving the courthouse, we arrived at the jail. A maximum-security, one-story, concrete building, the jail is located just below Seven Locks Road in a shallow ravine. The marshal who had cuffed me opened the back door and helped me get out and stand up.

He escorted me into the intake center at the back of the jail. Once inside, and after handing over some documentation to the officer and getting a receipt, he unfastened and removed my handcuffs. I was now in the custody of the Montgomery County, Maryland, jail system. Although I was not a county prisoner, the U.S. Bureau of Prisons contracts with local county jails to temporarily house federal prisoners while awaiting transfers to a federal facility. I didn't know how long I was going to be there or if or where I would be sent to serve out the six months of imprisonment Judge Gesell had imposed.

"Good luck," the marshal said as he turned and left.

"Thanks," I replied. I felt he meant it.

The intake officer and two other jail officials told me to go into a small room and take off my clothes. After one of them completed a body search, the other gave me a khaki shirt and pants to put on and directed me to keep my underwear and shoes and socks. I was taken from the intake room through a steel door and down a short hall to a temporary holding cell.

The holding cell was a rectangle about fifteen feet by twenty feet, with floor-to-ceiling bars on two sides and a heavy barred door set in one side. The officer unlocked the door and gestured me into the cell. A stand-up urinal was wedged in the corner, framed by mattresses on the floor shoved up against the walls. A Black man with a badly bruised face sat on the mattress to the right of the urinal and looked up at me as I stepped in. I heard the door clang shut behind me and the key turn in the lock. I had to choose where to sit.

Despite some fear, an inner impulse prompted me to walk over and sit down on the mattress next to the first cell occupant. Neither of us spoke for about a minute. We just sat there quietly. Finally, he raised his head, turned, looked at me out of the corner of his swollen eye, and said, "Krogh, I liked the way you did that. You just came over and sat down next to me. I know all about you. You're a stand-up guy. Now I'm going to teach you how to live in jail."

I looked at him as he said this. I was stunned and frightened that the first prisoner I met in jail knew my name and knew about my case. The odds were overwhelmingly stacked against such a coincidence, and I worried about what I might encounter later. He smiled at my shocked look and said that he had followed my case on TV. He then said he was going to give me some rules for surviving in jail.

The rules were basic and simple. Keep to yourself until you know the situation. Don't get in anyone's space or hide in a corner either. Don't look anyone directly in the eye right away until you know him, because it might be taken as a threat. Don't talk to the jailers or someone will think you're working for them and that's bad. He said, and I remember his words as if they were spoken yesterday: "You come in here as a white man, a lawyer, a Nixon dude. Don't you never hold yourself out better than anyone else in here. Don't do it because someone will hurt you if you do. And don't do it because it just ain't true."

These and other rules, a crash course in Jail Survival 101, flowed out of him over the next half hour. I asked about the daily routine, food, visitors, reading materials. He gave me good, helpful answers. A jailer came to the cell all too soon and summoned me to get up and follow him. I shook my friend's hand and thanked him, for he had extended himself in friendship to me, and followed the jailer out of the cell. I never saw him again.

The jailer led me out of the holding cell and down a corridor to a room stacked with mattresses, bedding, and towels. He told me to pick up a vinyl-covered mattress, sheets, and a towel. Carrying these items, I followed him to a larger detention unit in the back corner of the jail. He inserted his key in the steel door and directed me into a large cage-like cell that was to be my home for the next ten days.

This cell, with light-green walls and a dark-green floor, had three steel picnic-style tables and benches bolted to the floor, an open shower, two open commodes, and a sink in the first section. A television set was bolted to a steel platform about seven feet up near the steel door. Two rows of steel double bunks stretched into the back section of the cell. I walked to the end of the row of bunks on the right and tossed my mattress onto the top-bunk springs.

About ten men were in the cell, some at the tables watching television, a few in their bunks. No one acknowledged me as I walked in, and nothing was said. After

putting my sheets on the bed, I walked back to the near-
est table and found some open space on one of the steel
benches. Through the rest of the afternoon, we watched
television shows.

The evening news came on around five o'clock, and
one of the lead stories showed me, accompanied by my
wife Suzanne and my lawyer, Steve Shulman, turning myself in at the courthouse that morning. One fellow inmate
looked intently at the screen, back at me, then back to the
screen, then back at me.

"Man!" he said loudly. "I ain't seen no one WALK into
jail before!" This triggered interest from other prisoners
who now looked over at me.

"Why didn't you just take off?" he asked.

"Nowhere to go," I answered. I realized that in addition to other transient federal prisoners like me, some
of these inmates had been arrested at their crime scenes.
Taking off for them was a logical thing to do.

"I would have been easily recognized wherever I went.
Nowhere to run," I explained further. A couple of them
nodded their heads. When I explained the circumstances
of my case, one of them said I didn't belong there.

"Hey, man, you did what you thought was right. You
shouldn't be here."

This was dangerous ground, so I countered quickly
that I had pleaded guilty to a very serious crime. I explained that I had deprived a doctor of his right to be free
from an unwarranted search, a constitutional crime, and

that was serious stuff. I had to establish my mala fides as a criminal in order to have bona fides as a prisoner. And I applied one of the rules for survival that had just been given me a few hours before: "Don't you never hold yourself out better than anyone else."

Shortly after this conversation, a cart containing our dinners was wheeled outside of the cage, and steel trays were handed through a space in the bars. Each tray contained two cold hot dogs, some corn, bread, and a bottled beverage. I was more at ease that evening eating cold hot dogs off of a steel plate than I had been exactly one year before at my confirmation dinner in the White House. During that first evening in the Rockville jail, I recalled the imprisoning fear, pressure, and darkness that shrouded my mood during that White House dinner one year before. There, in the Rockville maximum-security jail, eating cold hot dogs off of a steel plate, I finally felt free, in harmony with myself, and at peace.

After ten days in the Rockville jail, I was transferred to Allenwood Federal Prison in White Deer, Pennsylvania, about two hundred miles north of Washington, D.C., in the foothills of the northern Allegheny Mountains. When I arrived there in mid-February 1974, handcuffed and foot-shackled, it was cold and bleak.

New prisoners at Allenwood were given the choice of working in a furniture factory, on the four-thousand-acre prison farm, in food preparation, or on the janitorial staff. At the recommendation of a fellow inmate at Rockville, I asked to be assigned to the Allenwood Farm. He had told me this would enable me to work outdoors. The kinds of farm jobs we did during a typical day included feeding some of the more than one thousand head of cattle, cleaning cattle pens, chopping underbrush, and clearing rocks. Later in the spring, after I had mastered the technique of operating the Massey Ferguson 1105 tractor, I plowed, disked, harrowed, and fertilized several of the fields where corn was to be planted.

During a typical day, I got up at the 6:00 A.M. count and then took my Bible and other spiritual literature to the small smoking room in the common area between the two dormitory wings where over 160 prisoners lived. There I studied and pondered the lives of those biblical figures who had "done time." I remember how moving the story of Joseph in the book of Genesis was to me. Rather than feel victimized by the terrible circumstances of his life—sold into slavery and imprisoned in Egypt—Joseph always tried to do his best and worked hard wherever he found himself. He didn't whine or complain. He took responsibility for his life. This story inspired me every day to give my best effort, whether working on the farm, helping other prisoners with their legal and family issues, or trying to stay fit by running around the dormitory compound.

Following this quiet time in the morning, I joined the farm crew for early breakfast and then piled on the truck that transferred us to the farm barns where our workday began. In the evenings I would read, answer letters, or counsel some of my fellow prisoners. The best part of each week for me was on Sunday when Suzanne and our two boys, Peter and Matthew, would drive the two hundred miles from our home in D.C. to spend three hours with me in the prison visiting room. I missed them terribly. They were always upbeat and lifted my spirits. Pete, in particular, was impressed that I had learned how to drive a tractor.

There is a before and after for every significant act we take and every choice we make. In the fifty years since the Watergate scandal, I pondered the reasons for those terrible decisions that took me to Rockville and Allenwood, and the lessons I learned from my time in the nation's capital and subsequent time in federal custody. Without my time in prison, I wouldn't have been able to answer for myself, and for this book, why good people make bad decisions, why we so often choose courses of action that inflict harm on those we would help, destroy our own careers, or undermine the institutions we serve. I had lost my way in the White House before prison, and afterward was the time to find my way home.

9

THE ROAD HOME

Just after midnight on June 22, 1974, I was released from federal custody. I had served the last two weeks of my prison sentence at Fort Holabird, Maryland, in a fenced two-story barracks tucked inside the military base. Most of the other prisoners in this facility were in the Justice Department's witness protection program. I was moved from Allenwood to Fort Holabird because the Watergate special prosecutor's office wanted me closer to Washington, D.C., so that they could get access to me quickly. They needed my testimony as part of their criminal cases for conspiracy against Ehrlichman, Liddy, and Hunt for their Plumbers offenses. In my plea of guilty on November 30, 1973, I had insisted that the court sentence me for my own crime before calling me to testify against any others on the White House staff. Special Prosecutor Leon Jaworski agreed to this condition if I would promise to testify truthfully when called as a prosecution witness. This I agreed to do.

After driving out of the gate at Fort Holabird, Suzanne and I decided it would be prudent to spend the night outside of the District. In those days, the press kept a watchful eye on the trial, imprisonment, and release dates of Nixon White House staff members, and we were not ready to meet the press in the middle of the night. Late the next morning, we pulled into our driveway at 6949 Greenvale Street N.W. in D.C. and were greeted by over a dozen reporters and cameramen. We spoke briefly to them, telling them how good it was to be home. When I walked into our house, I was greeted by a large sign that festooned the entrance that read, WELCOME BACK TO THE HOME OF THE BRAVE AND THE LAND OF THE FREE. Suzanne knew the exact right words for a great homecoming. Both my sons, Pete and Matt, were there jumping and running around, and we had a joyous reunion.

The next three weeks were spent getting familiar with freedom again. Many friends from all over the country called to tell us they loved us and were still pulling for us. Most of them knew that the ordeal of the inevitable attorney discipline proceedings lay ahead of us in Washington State. Bill Dwyer, the attorney in Seattle who had agreed to represent me in the Washington State Bar proceedings, informed us that a hearing was being planned for August 20, two short months away. He asked that we come to Seattle several days in advance to prepare.

Dwyer's acceptance of my case for the Washington Bar proceedings was pivotal to any future hope I had for practicing law again. Judge Gesell had acknowledged in his statement when sentencing me to prison that "you are standing at the Bar and hence your ability later to earn a living has already been undoubtedly adversely affected."

Six weeks before Judge Gesell sentenced me, I had met Dwyer for the first time. A close lawyer friend of mine, Keith Dysart, had called me right after I pleaded guilty to tell me that he had spoken with Dwyer and that he had agreed to meet with me. Keith told me Dwyer was viewed by many lawyers as one of the best litigating attorneys ever to practice law in Washington State. He added that Dwyer was a liberal Democrat, and he didn't know whether he would accept my case. I trusted Keith's judgment completely as he and I had practiced law briefly together in Ehrlichman's law firm before I left for the White House staff. Keith and I remained close friends over the next few years, so I was confident that if he felt Dwyer was the best lawyer for me, it would be true.

I called Dwyer's office and found out that he would be in Kalamazoo, Michigan, in mid-December 1973 taking depositions on a large antitrust case involving mint growers in Washington State. His secretary arranged for us to meet for two hours in downtown Kalamazoo at a café he frequented.

A few days later I flew up to Kalamazoo in a small commuter plane that was buffeted around in blizzard conditions. When we were seated and had ordered lunch, he sat back, smiled, and said, "OK, Bud, I've been reading about you in the papers. Keith asked me to meet with you, and I'm happy to do so. But I'd like to hear your story as you see it."

Feeling a great sense of trust and kindness from him, I spoke for about forty-five minutes. I gave him an account of the Plumbers' operation concluding with a full explanation of the reasons I had felt compelled to plead guilty to depriving Lewis Fielding of his civil rights. For the next hour, he asked questions that I answered as fully as I could. His questions were direct and designed to get me to open up my deepest feelings. It was a most gentle form of cross-examination, and he took my case.

He warned me that a prison sentence was likely, and he was, of course, right. He did not feel it was appropriate for me to "capitalize" on the serious constitutional crime that I had committed, so he urged me not to write a book right away that would make money. He said it would be important for me to make amends for my actions, and we would work together to find out how best to do that.

After my return home from prison (hardly a major news story), press interest shifted quickly to the upcoming trials of my former White House colleagues. The actual experience of testifying against Liddy and Hunt, two men who had worked for me, and especially against

Ehrlichman, my mentor and friend, was absolutely excruciating. Young, my codirector of the White House Plumbers, was given full immunity by Earl Silbert, the U.S. attorney who had initial responsibility for the Watergate cases. Young's immunity was offered in exchange for the Plumbers' documents and incriminating testimony he would provide later at the trials of Ehrlichman and other defendants. The prosecutors said my testimony was of great value because I had already served a prison sentence. While I had not received immunity, I was still obligated to testify truthfully as part of the plea agreement I had reached with Jaworski the previous year.

When I was on the stand as a prosecution witness, the prosecutors led me through a series of questions about the authority Young and I had received from Ehrlichman to carry out a covert operation. I was asked to confirm my initials on the memo from Young and me to Ehrlichman that recommended the operation. In answer to a question on cross-examination, I affirmed that at the time the Plumbers were operating in 1971, I felt that we were carrying out a mission dictated by a national security requirement. To a question posed by the prosecutor, I said that I had since changed my view and no longer felt that national security could justify what was done. My time on the stand was short—no longer than two hours—and it was a relief to have it over with. One of the most difficult things I have ever had to do in my life was to testify against my friends in a criminal trial. I had little doubt that they would be convicted and would serve prison sentences, and so it proved. Like me, they were convicted, and they did serve.

After concluding my testimony, Suzanne and I decided we should take a trip around the country and arrive in Seattle in time to prepare for the first hearing before the bar association panel. But first, we wanted to do something fun with our children. Like many who have gone through challenging times, we decided we should go to Disney World. On the way, we would pick up a cartoon.

During my term at Allenwood, a color cartoon by Ralph Dunagin was pinned up on the prison bulletin board. It depicted an obviously new prisoner sitting on a cot with an older con looking down at him and saying, "Eagle Crow, huh? Say, you're not the famous birdman of Alcatraz, are you?" This led to my being nicknamed "Birdman" by some fellow prisoners. I wrote Dunagin and asked if he would consider giving me the original. He wrote back and said that if I came to his newspaper in Orlando, Florida, after my release from prison, he would be delighted to give it to me.

For a few days we kicked back, rode all the rides we could at Disney World, marveled at the acrobatic tricks of whales and dolphins at Marine World, and caught up with my Orlando friends. During the previous year since my case had become public, generous financial support from hundreds of my fellow Principia College alums had come to us. Alumni from Principia, my undergraduate alma mater, are fiercely loyal to their own, and they live all over the United States and in many other countries. My close friend Jim Morand established the Bud Krogh Legal Defense Fund on my behalf along with Dick Nordahl, a fellow Principia graduate. To pay my legal fees, which ran into the tens of thousands of dollars even without a trial, Suzanne and I exhausted all our personal financial resources, including my small retirement account from the federal government. The legal defense fund paid for most of the remaining legal bills. I am eternally grateful to those who helped me so much in a time of extraordinary need.

After leaving Orlando, we drove across the country by the southern route, through Alabama, Mississippi, Louisiana, and Texas. We camped several nights in New Mexico and Arizona and arrived in Seattle in late July. Driving across large swaths of America released me from my previous preoccupation with the Watergate scandal and the imprisoning political perspective of Washington, D.C. With my family, I was able to relax and deeply enjoy the greatness, simplicity, and authenticity of that part of America that on the East Coast is often referred to as "flyover country."

As a boy and later as a law student, I had always enjoyed mountaineering. I dreamed of climbing Mount Rainier, a 14,410-foot volcano an hour away from Seattle. Suzanne and I persuaded my brother-in-law, Don Davis, and two of my nieces, Joelyn and Tishy Davis, to join us in training for a Rainier climb soon after we arrived in Seattle. I also planned to work closely with Bill Dwyer to prepare for the first hearing before the Washington State Bar Association's three-lawyer panel on whether I could continue to practice as a lawyer.

On August 8, 1974, a few days after taking a mountaineering course with Suzanne, my brother-in-law, and my two nieces, we left Mount Rainier's Paradise Lodge with our guides from Rainier Mountaineering Incorporated and headed up the mountain.

Through the night, our team rest-stepped slowly up the standard route on Rainier, crossed the Cowlitz and Ingraham Glaciers, and then went up Disappointment Cleaver. (If ever there was a name of a climbing route designed to discourage and sap the energy of aspiring summit climbers, "Disappointment Cleaver" was it.) Our group zigzagged back and forth, avoiding deep crevasses, and eased onto the eastern summit rim around 7:00 A.M., where we celebrated by drinking pints of water, eating dried fruit, salami, and cheese, and signing the register.

Our descent was slow, as it usually is for first-time climbers of Mount Rainier. On the last section of the descent, a couple of miles above the end of the climb at Paradise Lodge, we saw and then heard another party of about a dozen climbers heading up. As we got closer, we heard them yelling, "We have a new president! We have a new president! Nixon's gone! Ford's in! Nixon's gone! Ford's in!"

"What did you say?" I yelled over to them.

"Nixon just resigned. He's goooooone!!!" one of them yelled back gleefully.

I stopped in my tracks, took off my pack, and bent over. I was physically tired, but I now felt a huge emotional weight of sadness and regret. My family gathered around, and we just stood quietly together for a few minutes. Right then, standing on a snow field on Mount Rainier, I decided that it was time to complete some of the unfinished aspects of my earlier decision to take responsibility for my actions as head of the Plumbers. My actions had directly damaged at least two people, Ellsberg and Nixon. I had to make amends. And, no matter how difficult, I would have to do it in person.

10

MAKING AMENDS, AND A FINAL PARTING

With a guilty plea before Judge Gesell and a prison term served as honorably as I could, I had finished paying the minimum debt to society that had been required of me. For the sake of my own integrity and peace of mind, however, I felt the need to make amends to the men whom my actions had damaged the most. This would require me to go to California to apologize to Dr. Lewis Fielding and then to San Clemente to see Nixon.

The impact that I had on Dr. Fielding weighed heavily on me since the break-in and during my time in prison, when the importance of privacy and individual rights became abundantly clear. I had violated both Fielding's privacy and his rights, and I now had much more experience of what that could mean on a personal level. Prison, no matter how honorably one serves, is designed to deprive inmates of precisely both these things. The integrity of our society rests in part on the need to trust citizens to act with respect for each other's rights; in prison, that trust is revoked, and I felt the loss keenly, as I was sure Fielding had.

With Nixon, I needed to explain exactly what had happened with the SIU and my part in it. Many have reviled Nixon, then and now, as at best a ruthless politician, at worst an evil man who directed the scandals perpetrated during his presidency. For me, however, he was an important authority figure who often made clear, sometimes brilliant, policy decisions. In the areas that I directly worked on for Nixon—drug control policy, transportation, the District of Columbia—he had provided me with the ability to make decisions and changes that I felt were important and beneficial. I owed him both thanks and an apology for the impact my actions had on his presidency.

On August 22, 1974, I flew to Los Angeles, rented a car, and found a room in a motel near Beverly Hills. Up to that point, all the steps I had taken to accept responsibility and atone for what I had done as head of the Plumbers were in the public arena. I had pleaded guilty, explained to the court what had happened and why, and served a prison sentence. But I had not apologized to or expressed any remorse directly to Dr. Fielding, the victim of that crime. I saw that he was not "collateral damage," but an individual person harmed by me. The break-in and ransacking by the Plumbers of Fielding's office was a direct and personal assault on his property. The public exposure of the Plumbers' actions had thrust him into the glare of the public spotlight for a while. From what I could tell in reading about him in the press, he was quiet, reserved, and prized his privacy. I had concluded that simply pleading guilty to depriving Dr. Fielding of his civil rights and serving a prison sentence was insufficient if I was serious about taking full responsibility for what I had done. A moral debt to him was required.

I arrived at his low-rise office building in Beverly Hills around 1:00 P.M. and went upstairs to his office. It was closed and locked. After waiting in the corridor for about a half hour, I wondered whether it would have been a good idea to have called and made an appointment. I hadn't called because I wasn't confident that he would agree to see me. But I was so eager to tell him I was sorry, I was willing to risk his displeasure at showing up without an appointment.

A few minutes later I saw him—a slender, bald man with sharp features—walking down the hall. As he approached his office door, I walked over to him and said, "Excuse me, Dr. Fielding, my name is Bud Krogh, and I was wondering if I could speak to you for a few minutes." He looked at me with wide eyes, stepped back, recovered, nodded, and then stuck out his hand to shake my extended hand. "Oh, hello, Mr. Krogh. What did you want to speak to me about?" he said.

"Well, sir, I just wanted to come and tell you how

sorry I am about what we did to you. It was inexcusable and I want you to know that."

He looked at me for a moment, inserted the key into the door lock, and said, "Please, come in. I have a few minutes before my next appointment." I followed him into his office and, at his invitation, sat down. He then said, "I'm not surprised you are here. I've read a lot about you." I then told him I had been released from prison two months earlier, and that I had wanted to come see him as soon as I could. I told him I felt partly responsible not only for what had happened to him but also to the president and his administration. He listened quietly and then told me that he could accept my apology, but that I might have additional work ahead to get peace of mind. We talked a short while longer, and then his next appointment arrived and it was time for me to go. He walked me to the door and stuck out his hand. I shook it, thanked him, and we nodded at each other. I felt relieved of a great burden when I walked out of his office and very thankful to him for his kindness, grace, and understanding.

After my meeting with Dr. Fielding, I drove down the coast to San Clemente and got another motel room. Following my request for a time to meet with former president Nixon on August 24, Ron Ziegler, the former White House press secretary and now the top staff person in the San Clemente office, had scheduled me for an hour at 10:00 A.M. The next morning, when I drove through the Secret Service security check point on the way to the president's office, I was struck by how quiet and bleak everything felt. When the president vacationed in San Clemente in the past, there had always been a high level of energy, but not that day. When I arrived, it was silent and placid.

The view from the San Clemente office out to the Pacific Ocean was just as spectacular as I remembered it from previous visits. Just a short three years before, I had come to this office to be given the assignment by Ehrlichman to head up the Special Investigations Unit. I reflected on how much deep and troubled water had flowed under the bridge since then.

When I walked in, the first person I met was Ken Khachigian, one of the savviest political minds on the Nixon staff and a very good friend. Ken had worked down the hall from me in the Old Executive Office Building. Ken told me that he had signed on to help the president research and write his memoirs. I also saw Diane Sawyer, a former aide to Ron Ziegler in the press office who, like Ken, had joined the San Clemente staff to help with the memoirs. Diane was brilliant and funny. An indefatigable worker, she demonstrated a high degree of personal loyalty to the president by moving to California to work for him. Her successful career in broadcasting after leaving San Clemente is a result of her huge talent and intellect. I then spent a short time with Ron Ziegler, who told me that while the president was functioning well, he was still fragile. The president and everyone there were still numb and in a state of shock. He hoped that

I wouldn't be saying anything that would disturb him more. I told him I just wanted to give him some support, and that I was pulling for him. With that, he got up and led me over to the president's office.

Nixon and I shook hands. He was wearing a dark business suit with an American flag lapel pin, looking considerably older than I remembered him. His face was flushed; his eyes were bloodshot.

He looked exhausted.

I began by telling him that I was grateful for the chance to see him. I told him the Washington State Bar Association had determined (or, rather, the hearing panel had recommended) that I not be disbarred but suspended for a period of nine months.

He said he was glad they had only recommended suspension, and that the California Bar was contemplating some action with respect to him, but that he didn't care what they did. "I don't give a damn about that."

I said that I felt given a new lease on life, and that I was very appreciative of the help so many had given me during the hearing.

He asked me, "Do you have any plans now?" I told him that first I was going to return to the District of Columbia for a while. My wife was going to start teaching school around the first week of September, and we had to be back by that time. I said I hoped to do some teaching. When he asked me where, I mentioned that I had been contacted by Paul Hartman, a professor at Florida Technical Institute.

He said, "That's a great school. I gave a commencement address there. Great school."

I also said that I had been contacted by a person at Indiana University and someone working with a speakers' program at Mount Holyoke.

"That's great," he said.

I told him I hoped he knew how much good was accomplished in his administration.

He said, "Well, there were some good things and some bad things."

I said, "Yes, that's true, but you can't dwell completely on the bad."

He said, "Well, I've said, 'This scandal is the broadest but also the thinnest scandal.' . . . Well, it's all finished now."

In an effort to give him some comfort, I told him that he didn't have to accept that all was finished. I said that I had been afraid of what might happen to me when the indictments were handed down the previous year, but when I finally faced up directly to what I had done and had taken responsibility for my actions, I was able to see a course to get through the legal tangle. I told him I had seen him come back from hopeless circumstances in the past, and his example had been very helpful to me.

I also told him that in prison I had a choice about how

I was going to do my time. "Look," I said, "I could have decided to just sit over in a corner of my cell block or just sit against the wall in the prison camp and play my guitar, but I didn't do that. I learned how to plow, and tried to be the best plowman I could. I had to learn how to work with my hands. They got cut up. But I learned. I had to take the circumstance as I found it and go from there." I described how I had to see each prisoner there as a man who deserved my respect regardless of what he had done. He nodded to me as I said these things.

He was interrupted by a call from vice-presidential nominee Nelson Rockefeller. Nixon said, "I'm glad they've got you. You've got a lot of clout. . . . No, I'm not just being nice. It's true. . . . I appreciate what you said the other day. Did they give you a hard time about it? Yeah, well, I just don't think it would be good for the country to have a former president dumped in the D.C. jail." There was some more conversation, and then Nixon said, "Well, good-bye. Give our best to Happy." Then he hung up.

He said he felt responsible for my actions and asked me whether I thought he should plead guilty. I asked him whether he felt guilty, and he said, "No, I do not."

I told him that pleading guilty to a federal crime wasn't a public relations move, that you had to accept that you had committed a crime. I said there was a line between legal culpability and overall responsibility. I had determined that I was legally responsible and had to face it. I said I appreciated very much his saying that he felt responsible for what had happened. Finally, I said that I wanted him to know that I cared for him, and that I wanted to help him in any way I could (as, indeed, I had clearly stated in my letter of resignation to him).

Throughout my conversation with Nixon, I was mindful of Ziegler's admonition before going in to see him that Nixon was in a fragile state and that he hoped I would not say anything to disturb him further. I was feeling great compassion for him, so I did not press him on his legal guilt. But when he told me he did not feel guilty, I knew that he would not be able to acknowledge criminal liability. As he walked me to the door, he put his hand on my shoulder. We shook hands and wished each other well.

11

CLOSURE

Over the next two weeks, after my trip to Beverly Hills and San Clemente, I worked on a long memo that I intended to send to Nixon. I felt I hadn't been able to go into the detail necessary to explain my reasoning about taking responsibility. The main point I made in that draft memo was that as he worked through these days, he needed to face exactly what had happened. I didn't spell out how he should do this, but I described in detail my own experience as an example. In looking at the evidence against him, it appeared overwhelmingly clear to me that he had obstructed justice on numerous occasions after the Watergate break-in. The evidence amassed against him by the House Judiciary Committee during its impeachment inquiry over an eight-month period was very compelling. More evidence would have been developed by the special prosecutor and grand jury if a case against him had proceeded.

During and right after my meeting with him on August 24, 1974, I felt that if Nixon had been willing to face up to and plead guilty to what he had done as a matter of law, he had it within his grasp to affirm one of the most basic principles in the American legal system—that no man is above the law. I was also confident that if he had taken this path, he would not have been sentenced to a prison where he would have been at risk. But when he said he did not feel guilty of any crime, it was clear that he felt either that he had not broken any law, or if he had, it didn't apply to him because as president he was, indeed, above the law.

I never sent my memo to him because on September 8, 1974, President Gerald Ford "granted . . . a full, free, and absolute pardon unto Richard Nixon for all offenses against the United States which he, Richard Nixon, has committed or may have committed or taken part in during the period from January 20, 1969, through August 9, 1974." Ford's pardon rendered completely moot anything I was going to point out in my memo urging him to face exactly what had happened in terms of his own legal culpability. He would have the opportunity to face what had happened in writing his memoirs, but such reflection would not be compelled by the threat of any criminal prosecution.

Although Ford's pardon of Nixon could certainly be justified as a humane and compassionate act, and as a necessary step to avoid the inevitable national trauma of a protracted investigation and trial of Nixon, it had the effect of depriving Nixon of the opportunity to face up clearly to what he had done. The pardon was also a major cause of the defeat of Gerald Ford in the 1976 election against Jimmy Carter. And at a very basic level, a pardon leaves things unfinished, making it hard to get traction to move forward.

While serving as deputy counsel to the president in 1969, I was occasionally asked to review a high-profile application for presidential clemency submitted to the pardon attorney at the Department of Justice. I became convinced that a pardon or commutation of a prison sentence should be granted only to correct a mistake in a legal process, to serve a humanitarian need, or to acknowledge great service to society in the period after an applicant's release from custody. Because a pardon essentially sets aside the results of a legal process, it should be granted only sparingly.

The year before, I had dealt with the possibility of a presidential pardon from Nixon. Ehrlichman told me that after I resigned from the government, he had a conversation with Nixon and pressed the president to offer clemency to me if the need arose. Later in the year, after I decided to plead guilty to the civil rights charge, I had lunch with David Eisenhower at George Washington University. I told him I felt very strongly that if upon pleading guilty I was sentenced to prison, I did not want any clemency from the president. If a prison sentence was imposed, that was an essential part of taking responsibility for my decision. David told me later that when he was at Camp David with President Nixon and their families, the president decided to grant me a full pardon. David said he reached over to the president—whose hand was on the telephone—and asked him not to do it. "Let Bud work this out in his own way." I was grateful to David for sparing me the embarrassment of having to turn down a presidential pardon if it had been offered.

I felt then, and I do today, that a presidential pardon would have been disastrous for me. Many members of the bar in my home state had expressed grave concern about the negative effect on the reputation of the legal profession by the criminal convictions of so many law-yers in the Watergate scandals. A pardon for me from President Nixon would have exacerbated that sense of betrayal and, I believe, ended any chance of my working as a lawyer again.

After the three-lawyer panel recommended a relatively short nine-month suspension, the jubilation Bill Dwyer and I had felt was short lived. Within just a few weeks after the August hearing, the full board of governors met in closed session. I testified at length and responded to questions for the better part of a day.

After a short review, the board rejected the panel's rec-ommendation for a nine-month suspension and voted to recommend disbarment to the Washington State Supreme Court. Following a hearing before the full court in January 1975, the court issued an opinion in June ordering that I be disbarred. The vote was 7 to 2 in favor of disbarment, with very strong opinions written on both sides.

As permitted by court rules, two years later, in 1977, Bill and I applied to the board of governors for reinstatement. Again, there was a lengthy hearing, but the board did not support our petition for reinstatement and explained to us during the closed hearing that not enough time had elapsed from the court's earlier decision to disbar.

We had a decision to make. We were entitled to appeal the board's decision not to support reinstatement to the bar. However, Bill's strongly held opinion was that we needed to take the long-term view and consider the consequences of proceeding to the court without the full support of my professional association. If I wanted to be accepted by my future colleagues at the bar, it would be much better to go forward with the bar association's full support rather than its opposition. Taking the long view was one of the cardinal points Bill had insisted on when he had first taken my case in December 1973. We decided not to appeal.

Two years after that, in 1979, we again petitioned the board of governors for reinstatement, and this time the board concurred. It was a much different setting than the first court hearing in 1975. Not only was the political atmosphere different, but I had remarried and settled once again in Washington. Reinstatement to the

Washington Bar meant I could once again make a living practicing law, if only in Washington State.

This second time, Kurt Bulmer, the bar counsel, argued strongly before the court in favor of my reinstatement. With Bulmer's full support and Bill Dwyer's quiet yet passionate arguments on my behalf, the court heard a powerful case in favor of reinstatement. The court hearing was held in Olympia, the state capital, about sixty miles south of Seattle. Bill had spent the entire night before at his mother's bedside at the hospital, where she was gravely ill. During the drive to Olympia, he was able to rest for about a half hour. When our case was called, he gave the most eloquent reasons why I should be reinstated: it was a labor of immense dedication and compassion. In May 1980, four months after the hearing, the court voted 7 to 2 to reinstate me pending my passing the full bar examination. I took the exam in July and was formally sworn in to the practice of law the second time on October 22, 1980.

During my banishment from law between 1975 and 1980, I had to find a way to support our family while we were still in D.C., and also later, when I moved to California and Suzanne and the boys moved to Oregon. Occasional opportunities to teach and to give lectures on college campuses helped supplement the teacher's salary Suzanne was earning before we left D.C. In the spring of 1975, Congressman Paul N. "Pete" McCloskey called me up and invited me down to his office in the Longworth

House Office Building. When I walked in, he asked me how things were going.

"Well," I answered, "I'm not waiting beside the phone hoping that the White House will call and offer me a job." He laughed and asked if I would ever consider working with the legislative branch. "Yes, sir," I answered. He chuckled and then asked if I would consider working for the House of Representatives. "Yes, sir," I answered again, wondering where this was going. "Bud, would you consider working for me?" I was overwhelmed. "Absolutely, I would. It would be a great privilege!"

He led me into the adjoining office, where his administrative assistant and public information staff member had their desks. He pointed to a vacant desk with a lone file on top in the corner. "There's your desk. Fill out the forms in the file, and then let's go downstairs and get you a pass."

So began my second federal job, a brief tenure, for a man I deeply respected and admired. Some people rescue dogs and cats. McCloskey rescued people. During the time I worked with him, I heard many stories about people who had fallen on hard times whom he had helped. Hiring me at the time when the Watergate debacle was still a fresh wound in the minds of most Americans took tremendous moral courage. He was a physically courageous fighting marine during the Korean War, and he was a morally courageous public servant throughout his terms in Congress.

He was also brilliant, funny, and irreverent. The inscription to me in his gripping book *The Taking of Hill 610* reads, "To Egil 'Himself' Krogh, the most honest scoundrel I know, Pete McCloskey."

For the next eight months, I worked on McCloskey's staff in Washington, D.C., and back in his district in Palo Alto, California. My areas of responsibility included merchant marine matters, Russian competition in shipping, and transportation bottlenecks in McCloskey's district. It was interesting work, but I soon felt that it was time to try something completely new. During one of the periods I worked in the Palo Alto office, I fell in love with the Bay Area and decided it was time to leave Washington, D.C. This decision followed my disbarment in May 1975, when I realized that it would be a long time before I could return to the practice of law in Washington State.

So, in late 1975, I moved to San Francisco to begin a new life on my own. Years of accumulated stress from life in the capital, at the center of American government, had driven Suzanne and me apart a number of times. Coping with Watergate difficulties had briefly brought us closer together, but by late 1975 our marriage had reached a clear end. While I relocated to the Bay Area, Suzanne and the boys moved to Ashland, Oregon.

After a year of business in California, including my cross-continent commutes for Rep. McCloskey, an opportunity to make amends to a wider cross section of society presented itself. A close friend of mine, Tom

Fletcher, had served as the deputy mayor of D.C. for my first two years on the White House staff. Tom was an experienced, no-nonsense professional manager, and as the president's liaison with the District government, I had come to rely heavily on his judgment. When he left Washington for a position at Stanford Research Institute, we stayed in touch. I had told him of my decision to move to San Francisco.

One day he called me and asked me to have lunch with him and a close friend of his, Dr. Randy Hamilton, who was the dean of the Graduate School of Public Administration at Golden Gate University. We met for lunch at the grand old Palace Hotel on the corner of Montgomery and Market Streets. Dr. Hamilton was a droll, sprightly genius who regaled Tom and me with stories of his long and illustrious academic career. As we discussed some of my work in the White House, Dr. Hamilton turned to Tom and said, "Bud is going to teach one of our sections on public policy analysis next quarter." Tom and I looked at each other, very confused. This was the first we had heard about it.

"I am?" I asked, looking uncertain.

"Absolutely. You'll be great. First rate. Is this OK with you?"

"Yes, sir," I answered, "this will be great."

And so began my new career, a deeply satisfying one, of teaching public administration to graduate students at Golden Gate University. The work I enjoyed the most on the White House staff was converting public policy concepts into real, effective programs and designing the legislative, organizational, and budgetary systems that would implement those concepts. I had real-life experience in the world of public administration, and the focus of the Golden Gate University approach was the practical application of sound theory. For the next four and a half years, I taught public policy analysis, introductory public administration, values and conflicts in public management, and administrative law.

In the spring of 1976, the course I was teaching covered foreign policy. It was almost two years since I had last seen Nixon in San Clemente right after his resignation. In that period, he had weathered a near fatal bout of phlebitis, or inflammation of the veins that often coincided with blood clots (Nixon died later in 1994 from a severe stroke). After recovering, he worked hard at writing his memoirs. I called his office and asked if I could meet with him to get some insight on how best to present this section of the course.

On April 23, 1976, I met with Nixon from 11:45 A.M. to 1:10 P.M. He looked tanned, rested, and in good spirits. His brown eyes were clear and focused. He seemed to have recovered from the devastation of his resignation twenty months earlier. I thanked him for seeing me and told him that as I had mentioned to him at our earlier meeting, I was now teaching at the graduate level. I told him my focus in the course included the international narcotics program that I had responsibility for in the White House, but that I needed some understanding of how the other major elements of his foreign policy were approached.

He said, "You must have idealism and good public relations; but you also must have tough, even ruthless pragmatism to back it up." He stressed that a leader must understand the issues thoroughly. He said that he had traveled to every country; he understood how other leaders thought; and that this was where he felt his major contribution would be. After another hour or so, I thanked Nixon for his time. I think he felt some obligation to help me in my new teaching career.

In reviewing and typing up the notes from our meeting, I realized that he had given me some fairly basic and elementary ideas. Perhaps the comment that most illuminated his approach to policy, and probably government and politics generally, was the need for idealism and good public relations backed up with a "ruthless pragmatism."

For the next two years I taught full-time at Golden Gate University. I lived in the town of Mill Valley, five miles north of the Golden Gate Bridge in Marin County, where I spent my time running on Mt. Tamalpais and reading while my reinstatement hearings moved forward in

Washington State. As a refugee from the Watergate days, it was a time of recovery and reflection.

Bill Dwyer and I were very grateful for the support that Leon Jaworski, the former Watergate special prosecutor, had given to our cause in the two hearings before the three-lawyer panel and the board of governors. He had written letters arguing strongly that I was fit to practice law and urging that I be allowed back into the bar as soon as possible.

On October 16, 1978, Jaworski was to give a lecture on morality in government at the University of California, Berkeley, in Wheeler Auditorium. The main course I was teaching that quarter at Golden Gate University was values and conflicts in public management, for about twenty doctoral students. His subject and the course content fit perfectly, so I felt it would be a good experience for them to hear him.

When my students and I arrived at Wheeler Auditorium the hall was packed. We were able to find seats together for the class on the far right side of the hall. Over seven hundred students, faculty, and assorted Berkeley activists were jammed in. I wanted to see if I could visit briefly with Mr. Jaworski afterward to thank him for his support, so I wrote a note telling him that I was there with my class and asking if I could see him later. I walked up to the stage and handed it to a woman who appeared to be in charge. What happened over the next hour and a half painted an indelible memory for me, as my emotions ranged from stark terror to humble gratitude.

Jaworski wrote the following in an epilogue to his book *Confession and Avoidance*:

> As I walked into the auditorium, wedging my way through the students, one of my hosts handed me a note. I put the paper in my coat pocket and read it after I had taken my seat on the stage.
>
> The message was from the first White House aide to be indicted, and sentenced to prison, as a result of the Watergate crimes. He had lost his license to practice law and now taught a class in public administration at the university. His note, scrawled in black ink on a small square of memo paper, said he was in the audience with his students. He would like to say hello after my talk. He would understand if we could not.
>
> I was surprised, and pleased, and struck by more than a touch of irony. The topic of my speech was "Morality in Government." Even as I stood at the microphone, listening to my words echo in the quiet, my mind wandered to the note in my pocket and the man who wrote it. I was not sure what I would do, or even what I wanted to do.
>
> As I moved deeper into the points on Watergate, I instinctively stopped and departed from the text. I said, "One of the men who was involved in this case is in our audience tonight. His experience in government goes to the heart of this issue and what we can

learn from it. I must tell you that I have a high regard for him today. He is a man who acknowledged
his mistake and paid a price for it. What is more, he
asked for no favors or special privileges, from the
prosecutor or the court. He said he found his own
conduct indefensible and he was willing to take the
punishment for what he had done.

"I admire him," I went on, "for the manner in
which he accepted the responsibility for his actions.
I cannot say the same for his former employer, his
President."

As I paused, to look down at my speech and find
my place, I was aware of a murmuring in the crowd.
Later, in the question and answer period, a student
rose and asked, "Sir, would you mind identifying the
individual to whom you made reference during your
Watergate comments?"

I said, "No, I will not. That would be an invasion
of his privacy for me to single him out. He is here
as a member of this audience, as you are." I looked
around the room. "However, if he does not object to
making his presence known, I would leave it to him
to do so. If he is willing to be recognized, this would
be an appropriate time."

Heads turned and craned. Time seemed to freeze
as I waited. I did not even know if he was still in the
room, or where he was seated.

Then, off to my left, there was a stir. Not in a bouncy, proud way, but slowly, with some reluctance, he climbed to his feet and looked around uncertainly.

I nodded, made a quick gesture with my left hand and said, "This is Egil (Bud) Krogh."

The auditorium vibrated with applause, a sound that swelled and grew and slapped off the walls. The ovation must have lasted two or three minutes. I do not know how many political rallies I have attended, although the number is too many, but I have never seen or heard anything quite as genuine as the emotion that crowd gave to Bud Krogh, an ex-lawyer who had just been introduced by the man who sent him to prison . . .

After the program ended, and I stood chatting at the podium and even signing autographs, Bud Krogh appeared at my side. All we said was hello, but we shook hands and our eyes caught and, at that moment, I felt a flicker of hope. The enduring question of Watergate is whether we, as a people, will learn from it. Some have.

When Jaworski indicated during his speech that now would be a good time for me to be recognized, I was struck with terror. Here I was, with my class, at the epicenter of the radical movement in America. I didn't believe there was one person in that hall who had voted for

Nixon. Would I be attacked? I looked over at my students, who were glancing at me with worried faces. One of them pointed to a side exit if we had to escape quickly. But I felt, too, that not to acknowledge Jaworski's gracious offer to recognize me would be rude and cowardly. So I got up, very slowly, so that I could gauge how bad things could get. I was dumbfounded by the overwhelming applause that erupted, and I must attribute most of it to the high respect that audience felt for Jaworski.

In discussing this experience later with my students, we acknowledged how important it is to own up to our mistakes and not try to blame others for our own errors. This was a theme that was emphasized in the courses I taught over the next two years before returning to Seattle. Again and again, the importance of taking responsibility for one's actions emerged as a vital life principle.

After reinstatement to the Washington Bar on October 22, 1980, I joined Bill Dwyer's law firm in Seattle. I practiced law at Culp, Dwyer, Guterson & Grater for the next fifteen years before going out on my own as a lawyer. For the first time since 1968—when I left Seattle for Washington, D.C.—I had returned home to my place, my profession, and a semblance of stability.

Just over ten years after meeting President-elect Nixon, and after accepting a job with my long-time mentor John Ehrlichman, my White House journey concluded. What had begun as a youthful opportunity filled with ambition had come crumbling down. While I had started that

White House path together with Nixon, we had finally parted ways. My prison sentence based on a plea of guilty gave me the opportunity to atone in ways that he and so many others involved in the administration could have benefited from.

TIMELINE

NOVEMBER 5, 1968
Richard M. Nixon wins the presidential election. Spiro Agnew is his vice president.

JANUARY 20, 1969
Nixon is inaugurated as the thirty-seventh president of the United States.

JUNE 13, 1971
The New York Times starts publishing excerpts of the Pentagon Papers.

JULY 17, 1971
John Ehrlichman meets with Krogh in San Clemente, telling Krogh that POTUS has ordered an independent team to investigate the leak of the Pentagon Papers.

JULY 19, 1971
Back in D.C., Krogh calls G. Gordon Liddy.

JULY 20, 1971
Liddy joins the White House staff.

JULY 21, 1971
E. Howard Hunt introduces himself to the unit, having been assigned by Chuck Colson. Krogh calls FBI director Hoover for polygraph tests.

JULY 23, 1971
First meeting of the Special Investigations Unit (or SIU) that would come to be known as the Plumbers: Krogh, Young, Liddy, Hunt, Chenow. *The New York Times* publishes an article revealing U.S. strategy for SALT I talks.

JULY 24, 1971
Nixon calls a meeting.

JULY 29, 1971
Nixon sends a letter to Hoover about the SIU's mission.

AUGUST 2, 1971
Liddy sends a memo about the FBI.

AUGUST 3, 1971
Hoover acknowledges receipt of Nixon's letter and sends a background paper on Ellsberg to Krogh.

AUGUST 11, 1971
Krogh and Young draft a memo to Ehrlichman recommending a covert operation to examine the files of Ellsberg's psychiatrist and psychoanalyst, Dr. Lewis Fielding. Ehrlichman approves.

AUGUST 25, 1971
Liddy and Hunt leave for California and check into the Beverly Hilton hotel.

AUGUST 26, 1971
Liddy and Hunt survey Dr. Fielding's office.

SEPTEMBER 1, 1971
Cash is delivered to Krogh to cover the operation.

SEPTEMBER 3, 1971
The operation goes forward: Hunt's team—Bernard Barker, Felipe de Diego, and Eugenio Martinez—break into Dr. Fielding's office.

SEPTEMBER 5, 1971
Hunt and Liddy return to D.C.

SEPTEMBER 7, 1971
Krogh meets with Liddy, sees photos of the break-in.

SEPTEMBER 8, 1971
Krogh shows Ehrlichman the photos. They agree this is beyond the scope of the mission. Krogh reports back to Liddy and Hunt that Ehrlichman rejects the suggestion to break into Fielding's apartment. Krogh's involvement with the covert activities of the Plumbers end.

SEPTEMBER 9, 1971
Ehrlichman meets with Nixon and tells him all he needs to know about the "little operation in California."

SEPTEMBER 10, 1971
Ehrlichman meets with Nixon and recommends another covert operation, this time into the National Archives.

DECEMBER 1, 1971
Liddy leaves the SIU and the White House and goes to CRP.

JUNE 19, 1972

Krogh learns of a break-in at the Watergate Hotel.

AUGUST 28, 1972

Krogh lies to a grand jury during the Watergate investigation.

FEBRUARY 4, 1973

Krogh and his wife dine with Nixon in the State Dining Room of the White House to commemorate his move to the Department of Transportation.

MAY 2, 1973

Krogh resigns his position of undersecretary of transportation.

OCTOBER 11, 1973

Krogh is indicted for lying to the Watergate grand jury.

NOVEMBER 30, 1973

Krogh pleads guilty to Fourth Amendment violations before the special prosecutor for Watergate and related crimes, Leon Jaworski.

JANUARY 24, 1974

Krogh's sentencing hearing is held.

FEBRUARY 4, 1974

Krogh enters Montgomery County detention center in Rockville, Maryland.

FEBRUARY 14, 1974

Krogh transfers to Allenwood Federal Prison.

JUNE 22, 1974

Krogh is released from prison after two weeks at Fort Holabird.

AUGUST 8, 1974
Nixon resigns.

AUGUST 24, 1974
Nixon and Krogh meet in San Clemente.

JANUARY 1975
The Washington State Supreme Court recommends Krogh be disbarred.

APRIL 23, 1976
Krogh and Nixon meet again.

MAY 15, 1980
Washington Supreme Court votes to allow Krogh to be reinstated to the Washington State Bar.

OATH OF OFFICE (1966, PL 89–554)

An individual, except the President, elected or appointed to an office of honor or profit in the civil service or uniformed services, shall take the following oath: "I, AB, do solemnly swear (or affirm) that I will support and defend the Constitution of the United States against all enemies, foreign and domestic; that I will bear true faith and allegiance to the same; that I take this obligation freely, without any mental reservation or purpose of evasion; and that I will well and faithfully discharge the duties of the office on which I am about to enter. So help me God." This section does not affect other oaths required by law.

(Pub. L. 89–554, Sept. 6, 1966, 80 Stat. 424)

The President
The White House
Washington, D. C. 20500

Dear Mr. President:

As I have confirmed in an affidavit filed with the U.S. District Court in Los Angeles, I agreed to a certain mission by employees of the special investigative unit which operated under my direction from The White House in 1971. As the sworn statement makes clear, agreement to this mission was my responsibility, a step taken in excess of instructions, and without the knowledge or permission of any superior.

Under the circumstances which prevailed in the summer of 1971, and based on the best information available to me at the time, I believed that my decision was dictated inescapably by the vital, national security interests of the United States. I now see that this judgment may well have been in error, though prompted by what was then my highest sense of right. Its consequences, to my eternal regret, have proved injurious both to a number of innocent persons and to that reverence for law on which our society is founded.

My overriding desire now is to accept full responsibility for my acts and decisions and to assist in bringing all the facts and circumstances into the open so that a fair judgment of this activity can be rendered. With public confidence in our Government already shaken by the Wagergate affair, and with the complete affirmation of your personal integrity so imperative at this time, I cannot remain in the Administration while my role in the special investigative unit is submitted to the legal scrutiny it must now properly receive. It is right that the men and women of the Department of Transportation have an Under Secretary who enjoys full public trust and can devote full time to his job. It is for these reasons that I submit my resignation as Under Secretary of Transportation.

The opportunity I have had to participate in your Administration during the past four years has been the greatest experience of my life. In particular, it was rewarding for me as a member of your staff to have a hand in the establishment of your global program to combat narcotics and drug abuse, and to work closely with the people of the District of Columbia during this period of great progress for the City. My service at the Department of Transportation, though brief, has also brought priceless lessons and friendships with many superb public servants whom you can be proud to have on your team.

I leave the Government with great reluctance and sadness at the conclusion of a chapter that has meant so much, but also with the sincere hope that my actions in the coming days will contribute to the inexorable process of healing in which our country is now caught up. Truth alone can bring the healing and make men free, and as best I can I am making truth my guide. I am grateful beyond words for the privilege of serving with you, and would welcome any occasion the future might bring for me to assist you personally or to re-enter the service of the United States.

Respectfully,

Egil Krogh, Jr.

Statement of Egil Krogh, Jr.
to the Court (Hon. Gerhard Gesell)
Upon Entering Plea of Guilty

The sole basis for my defense was to have been that
I acted in the interest of national security. However, upon
serious and lengthy reflection, I now feel that the sincerity
of my motivation cannot justify what was done and that I cannot
in conscience assert national security as a defense. I am
therefore pleading guilty because I have no defense to this
charge. I will make a detailed statement as to my reasons
which I will submit to the Court and make public prior to
sentencing.

My decision is based upon what I think and feel is
right and what I consider to be the best interests of the
nation. The values expressed by your Honor in the hearing
on defense motions on November 13 particularly brought home
to me the transcendant importance of the rule of law over
the motivations of man.

I have expressed to the Special Prosecutor's office
my desire that I not be required to testify in this area until
after sentencing. My plea today is based on conscience, and
I want to avoid any possible suggestion that I am seeking
leniency through testifying. The Special Prosecutor's office
has expressed no objection to this position.

My coming to this point today stems from my asking
myself what ideas I wanted to stand for, what I wanted to represent to myself and to my family and to be identified with for

the rest of my experience. I simply feel that what was done in the Ellsberg operation was in violation of what I perceive to be a fundamental idea in the character of this country -- the paramount importance of the rights of the individual. I don't want to be associated with that violation any longer by attempting to defend it.

November 30, 1973

ACKNOWLEDGMENTS

Without the graceful and dogged determination of Laura Dail and her stellar team at Laura Dail Literary Agency, none of this would have happened, from the original *Integrity: Good People, Bad Choices, and Life Lessons from the White House* to this revision published as *The White House Plumbers*. A huge thank you to Hannah Phillips, our editor at St. Martin's Press, who along with Sally Richardson, Ginny Perrin, Bill Warhop, Jonathan Bush, Kelly Too, Lena Shekhter, and the entire production team, made this book such a fabulous final edition. And special thanks to my mom, Dr. Suzanne Krogh, and my brother Peter Krogh, for providing color commentary and memories to fill in essential details of the story.

INDEX

ABOUT THE AUTHORS

Egil "Bud" Krogh (1939–2020) made headlines as a Nixon administration official who went to prison for his role in what would lead to the Watergate scandal. He was a Navy veteran; a lawyer in Seattle, Washington; special assistant to the president; and undersecretary of transportation. In 1973, he pled guilty to "conspiracy against rights of citizens" for his role in the 1971 break-in at the office of Dr. Lewis Fielding and served four and a half months in prison. After serving his time, he rebuilt his reputation, resuming his law practice and speaking and writing on ethics. He was senior fellow on Ethics and Leadership at the Center for the Study of the Presidency and Congress and counselor to the director at the School for Ethics and Global Leadership in Washington, D.C.

Matthew Krogh (1970–) is a professional change maker focused on issues of climate change, fossil fuels, and policy. Mostly based in Bellingham, Washington, he has spent his career in nonprofit activism at various organizations, and has worked as a freelance writer, ranger, and geographic analyst. He is grateful for the opportunity to amplify his dad's important life lessons through co-authoring *The White House Plumbers,* along with its earlier iteration, *Integrity.*

Made in the USA
Middletown, DE
18 May 2024

54534212R00124